PUBLIC EDUCATION

PUBLIC
EDUCATION

━━

LAWRENCE A. CREMIN

FOREWORD BY MAXINE GREENE

━━

BASIC BOOKS, INC., PUBLISHERS

NEW YORK

The John Dewey Society Lecture—NUMBER FIFTEEN

The John Dewey Lecture is delivered annually under the sponsorship of the John Dewey Society. This book is an elaboration of the Lecture given in 1975. The intention of the series is to provide a setting where able thinkers from various sectors of our intellectual life can direct their most searching thought to problems that involve the relation of education to culture. Arrangements for the presentation and publication of the Lecture are under the direction of the John Dewey Society Commission on Lectures.

Library of Congress Cataloging in Publication Data

Cremin, Lawrence Arthur, 1925–
    Public education.

    (The John Dewey Society lecture; no. 15)
    1. Public schools—United States. I. Title.
II. Series: The John Dewey Society lectureship
series; no. 15.
LA212.C73   379.73   75-36376
ISBN 0-465-06775-1

CONTENTS

v

FOREWORD

IN the concluding section of *The Public and Its Problems*, John Dewey wrote:

We have but touched lightly and in passing upon the conditions which must be fulfilled if the Great Society is to become a Great Community; a society in which the ever-expanding and intricately ramifying consequences of associated activities shall be known in the full sense of that word, so that an organized, articulate Public comes into being.

Lawrence A. Cremin takes up the implied challenge in the present volume. His unifying theme has to do with the associated educational activities that take place in the multiple institutions of contemporary society. He writes of the ways in which these institutions relate to one another and engage with one another in "configurations of education," of the ways in which the education of the public presently proceeds. Comprehensive description of this kind is fundamental if we are to understand how experiences are mediated in the modern world, how values are identified and pursued, and how the demands of individuality are balanced with the demands of community. It is clearly fundamental if we are to understand at last "the conditions which must be fulfilled if the Great Society is to become a Great Community."

Working with Dewey's distinction between "schooling" and

"education," Professor Cremin expands the notion of intentional education and suggests that it takes place in families, churches, workplaces, publishing houses, and television stations, as much as it does in schools. This in no sense diminishes the significance of the schools: engaging with the many other educators in society, acknowledging the reality of "the intricately ramifying consequences" of their activities, the schools are described as playing an integral and vital role. Teacher education, similarly, is challenged in novel ways, the more "relational" and extensive becomes its concern.

A Deweyan spirit suffuses this book, even in its reevaluations. The "latitudinarian" descriptions continually open questions of assessment and evaluation; and the criteria brought to bear have to do with growth, self-education, and the ongoing search for community. The core concern throughout is, as it must be, with communication, with discussion in the public space. "Democracy," wrote Dewey, "will come into its own, for democracy is a name for a life of free and enriching communion." Lawrence Cremin has brought new vitality to the democratic conversation. The John Dewey Society is proud to open it to the public and invite the public to enter in.

MAXINE GREENE
Chairperson, Commission on Lectures
The John Dewey Society for the Study
of Education and Culture

PREFACE

———

AMERICANS have been living through a revolution in education during the past quarter-century that may be as profound as the development of the public schools more than a hundred years ago. It is a revolution compounded of several elements—the rapid expansion of higher education to a point where one out of every two high-school graduates has been going on to college; the massive shifts in population, from east to west, from south to north, from country to city, and from city to suburb, which have created new and extraordinary clienteles to educate; the movement of women into the labor force in unprecedented numbers, with prodigious consequences for the family; the changing character of work associated with the emergence of a postindustrial society, and in particular the rapid growth of the so-called knowledge industries; the various civil rights and liberation movements of the 1960s, which so radically changed the management and politics of education.

And beneath all of these—and relentlessly affecting them—has been the educational transformation wrought by mass television. In 1950, fewer than 10 percent of American homes had television sets. Today, the figure has leveled off at around 96 percent. Moreover, so far as can be determined, at least one member of the average American household is looking at a television set more than six hours out of every twenty-four, with the greatest amount of viewing being done by the very young, the very old, and the very poor. Once one recognizes that television teaches—and not only via channels specifically labeled educational but across the entire spectrum of public and commercial programming—the fact of television in 96 percent of American homes being looked at six hours a day is in itself a revolution. That revolution has drastically altered familial education. It has radically changed the education of the public at large. And it has fundamentally transformed the context in which all schooling proceeds.

The intent of the essays that follow is to sketch a theory of public education that takes account of these changes, using theory in its commonsense meaning as a systematic description or general statement of a field. The thrust of the argument is latitudinarian, the effort being to indicate the range and variety of institutions that educate the public and to which the public must therefore attend as it contemplates its own political development. Good theory serves many purposes at many levels, but at the least it should convey a sense of the richness and complexity of the phenomena it seeks to illumine. And it is precisely a sense of richness and complexity that has been missing from the educational discussions of recent years.

To this end, the first essay discusses the limitations of progressive educational theory in virtually confining its attention to the school and the relationships between school and society. My argument there is that progressivism became the mainstream of American educational thought during the middle decades of the twentieth century and that its limitations are now generic. The second essay proposes a revision of the progressive theory that seeks to detail the educational situation more fully and effectively. The third essay explores the implications of that revision for public policy making in education. And the fourth essay explores the bearing of that revision on the education of educators.

Parts of the first essay and most of the third were initially presented as an address to the John Dewey Society in February 1975. I should like to state my gratitude to the officers of that Society and to the members of its Commission on Lectures for the honor implicit in the opportunity. I had the good fortune of knowing John Dewey during the last years of his life and of conversing with him from time to time about some of the issues raised in these essays. He should not, of course, be held responsible for the outcome, but it might be useful for me to indicate that I see the ideas set forth here as essentially continuous with Dewey's, that is, within the spirit and framework of *Democracy and Education* (1916) and *The Public and Its Problems* (1927), though they also attempt the reformulations required by new circumstances.

Finally, it is a pleasure to express my appreciation to the Carnegie Corporation of New York for its continuing encouragement and support of my scholarly endeavors.

LAWRENCE A. CREMIN

SOME PROBLEMS IN
THE PROGRESSIVE THEORY
OF EDUCATION

━━━━━

THERE IS a fundamental problem in the progressive theory of education that I think bears scrutiny by those concerned with the politics of education in contemporary America. One can describe the problem in fairly technical terms, as the positing of a polarity between school and society that fails sufficiently to particularize the realities of the educational situation. Or one can describe it more simply, as the tendency to focus so exclusively on the potentialities of the school as a lever of social improvement and reform as to ignore the possibilities of other educative institutions.

The problem is discernible in many of the classic progressive treatises, most notably, perhaps, in John Dewey's *Democracy and Education* (1916). Recall Dewey's argument in the early sections of that work. The most important distinction be-

3

tween living beings and inanimate things, Dewey tells us, is that living beings maintain themselves by renewal. Among humans, that renewal takes place through a process of cultural transmission, which Dewey refers to as "education in its broadest sense." Education in its broadest sense is continuous, ubiquitous, pervasive, and all-powerful—indeed, so powerful that Dewey draws the moral that the only way in which adults can consciously control the kind of education children get is by controlling the environment in which they act, think, and feel.[1]

Then, in a crucial leap, Dewey goes on to tell us that there is a marked difference between the education everyone gets simply from living with others and the deliberate education offered by the school. In the ordinary course of living, education is *incidental*; in schooling, education is *intentional*. In developing the argument, Dewey takes the familiar progressive tack of going back to the origins of institutions in some primordial state of society. The family, he tells us, began in the desire to gratify appetites and secure the perpetuity of a line. Religious associations, he continues, began in the desire to ward off evil influences and obtain the favor of supreme powers. And organized work began in the simple enslavement of one human being to another. Any education that might have derived from participation in these institutions, he points out, was at best incidental. And, indeed, he indicates by way of illustration that savage groups have no special devices or materials or institutions for teaching the young, with the exception of initiation ceremonies. For the most part, they depend on

[1] John Dewey, *Democracy and Education* (New York: Macmillan, 1916), p. 3.

the kind of incidental learning that derives from shared activity.[2]

As civilization advances, however, life becomes more complicated, and much of what adults do is so complex that mere participation no longer assures the transmission of culture. At this point, Dewey suggests, intentional agencies, called schools, and explicit materials, called studies, come into being. And the task of transmitting particular aspects of life is delegated to a special group of people called teachers. Dewey is careful to point out that schools are an important means for transmitting culture, but only one means among many, and, when compared with other agencies, a relatively superficial means. Nevertheless, schools are the only means adults really have at their disposal for going systematically and deliberately about the education of the young.[3]

Once this leap is made, it is decisive in Dewey's argument. Though Dewey returns at a number of places to what he calls the "social environment," the remainder of the book is not about families, or churches, or work, but rather about schools. Dewey's theory of education is ultimately a theory of school and society. And while Dewey was primarily concerned with reconciling the dualism between school and society, I would stress the fact that he may have left us with the theoretical polarity in the very process of attempting the reconciliation. To say this is in no way to deny that the schools of Dewey's time were abstruse, formalistic, and in need of reconciliation with society. It is rather to suggest that Dewey may ultimately have

[2] Dewey, *Democracy and Education*, pp. 7–8.
[3] Dewey, *Democracy and Education*, pp. 8–9.

been victimized by the very polarity he set out to reconcile.[4]

That polarity had prodigious consequences for the discussion of education and politics during the 1920s and 1930s. We can see it in the two quite different arguments put forward within the progressive camp during the early years of the Depression. On the one hand, George S. Counts asked, "Dare the school build a new social order?" and called upon teachers forthrightly to indoctrinate children in the values of democratic socialism as their contribution to the development of a reconstructed American society. To Counts's argument, however, Dewey replied that whether or not teachers *dared* build a new social order in that particular way or some other, they probably *couldn't*. In a modern industrial society, with its multiplicity of political and educative agencies, the school could never be the main determinant of political, intellectual, or moral change. The best the school could do would be to form the understanding and the dispositions necessary for movement toward a changed social order.[5]

On the other hand, the group that prepared *The Educational Frontier*, of which Dewey was a member, went in the opposite direction. Far from daring the school to build a new social order, they despaired of the school making any appreciable difference whatever until the larger social ambience within which the school carried on its work had been fundamentally altered. Hence, Robert Bruce Raup called upon teachers to

---

[4] Dewey, *Democracy and Education*, pp. 12–27 and *passim*.

[5] George S. Counts, *Dare the School Build a New Social Order?* (New York: John Day, 1932); John Dewey, "Education and Social Change," *The Social Frontier* 3 (1936–37): 237, and "Can Education Share in Social Reconstruction?" *The Social Frontier* 1 (1934–35): 11–12.

enter the political lists and struggle for a better life in order to create a more hospitable and productive world in which to educate. "When the type of character desired by the school is so dependent for support upon conditions in the whole culture," Raup maintained, "and this support is not forthcoming, the educator's responsibility moves out into society to agitate and to work for that support." Here too, however, though Dewey was a working member of the yearbook committee, he demurred, contending that his advocacy of educators assisting in the development of a changed social order was in no way an advocacy of the school throwing itself into the political arena and taking the side of some particular party there.[6]

Now, my interest is only incidentally in locating Dewey with respect to the problem I have posed. It is primarily in explicating the problem itself. For, in the last analysis, the progressives ended up on the horns of a dilemma: they could either politicize the school, remaining dubious about their efforts, since the school was so powerless, or they could abandon the school and enter the political lists, seeking gradually or cataclysmically to change the entire social ambience in which youngsters came of age. Dewey revealed the dilemma beautifully in an address he gave to a conference on early childhood education at Teachers College in the spring of 1933. The address began with one of Dewey's great aphorisms: "The most utopian thing about utopia is that there are no schools at all." Education in utopia, Dewey went on to say, is carried out without benefit of schools, since children learn what they have

---

[6] William H. Kilpatrick, ed., *The Educational Frontier* (New York: D. Appleton-Century, 1933), p. 100; Dewey, "Education and Social Change," p. 236.

to know in informal association with the adults who direct their activity. So far, so good. But Dewey did not go on from that point to describe a utopian society whose values were so pervasive and whose institutions were so cohesive as to form the young through the very process of living. Rather, he went on to describe a society in which there were schools, but essentially activity schools of the sort he and his daughter Evelyn had written about in *Schools of To-Morrow* (1915). In 1933 Dewey was still trying to reconcile the dualism between school and society, but he was for all intents and purposes the victim of his own theoretical polarity. And, indeed, that polarity persists right down to the present time. We see it in the ambivalence of the educational reform movement of the 1960s, with its free-school proponents on the one side and its deschool proponents on the other. And we see it also—and in a more dangerous form perhaps—in the vast pendulum swing of American opinion during the 1970s, from a century-long overreliance on schooling as a general instrument of social aspiration to a widespread disenchantment with schooling. Whether or not we like Dewey and the progressives, we are heirs to their formulations, and the irony is that an age that has all but forgotten Dewey is still governed by his analytical categories.[7]

---

[7] Dewey's remarks were excerpted in *The New York Times*, April 23, 1933, under the heading "Dewey Outlines Utopian Schools." I am indebted to Jo Ann Boydston, Director of the Center for Dewey Studies at Southern Illinois University, for the reference.

II

IT IS ALMOST a commonplace to remark the continuities and similarities between the progressive education movement and the more recent educational reform movement of the 1960s, though, curiously, there has been a dearth of systematic writing on the subject. Like its earlier counterpart, the recent movement arose in protest against the widely perceived inadequacies and inequities of contemporary schools. Like its earlier counterpart, the recent movement was remarkably diverse, often self-contradictory, and closely related to broader currents of social and political reform. And, like its earlier counterpart, the recent movement embraced an extraordinary variety of participants, from militant equalitarians favoring highly structured programs to bring disadvantaged minorities into the educational mainstream, to moderate reformers committed to open schooling on the British model, to radical anarchists opposed to all structures because of their uncompromising belief in the sovereign wisdom of the child.[8]

One can date the recent movement from various beginnings, probably the most significant being the publication of A. S. Neill's *Summerhill* in 1960. The initial appearance of

[8] For examples of recent literature commenting on the relationship between the earlier movement and the later, see James R. Squire, ed., *A New Look at Progressive Education* (Washington, D.C.: Association for Supervision and Curriculum Development, 1972); Paul L. Houts, ed., "The Great Alternatives Hassle," *The National Elementary Principal* 52, no. 6 (April 1973); Lawrence A. Cremin, "The Free School Movement: A Perspective," *Notes on Education*, no. 2 (October 1973); and Robert Anderson and Thomas Hunt, "The Free School in America: Another Look," *Educare Journal* 3 (Spring 1975): 10–14.

the book, it might be noted, marked a singular nonevent in the history of American publishing. Nothing in it was new—Neill had written more than a dozen books on education and most of what he had recommended had been tried in one way or another in the progressive schools of the 1920s and 1930s. When the original publisher of *Summerhill* first announced the title, not a single bookseller in the country ordered an advance copy. Yet a decade later the book was selling at a rate of over 200,000 copies annually. Incidentally, 1960 was also the year in which Paul Goodman published *Growing Up Absurd*, with its call for the completion of "the missed and compromised revolutions of modern times," among them, the revolution called progressive education.[9]

However one resolves the question of precise beginnings, the movement developed slowly during its early phase, manifesting itself primarily in the organization of Summerhill societies and Summerhill schools in various parts of the country. It gathered momentum after mid-decade, fueled by the enthusiastic writings of John Holt, Joseph Featherstone, George Dennison, James Herndon, and Jonathan Kozol (whose *Death at an Early Age* won a National Book Award in 1968) and stimulated by the innovations of such educators as Leonard G. W. Sealey and Nora L. Goddard in England and Lillian Weber and John Bremer in the United States. And it peaked during the first years of the 1970s, when Allen Graubard could count several hundred free schools or new schools that had grown up "outside the system," and any interested ob-

[9] Paul Goodman, *Growing Up Absurd: Problems of Youth in the Organized System* (New York: Random House, 1960), pp. 217, 225.

server could enumerate literally thousands of schools, schools within schools, and classrooms within schools that were part of the public school system and variously referred to as alternative or open or informal programs.[10]

One element in the peaking was surely the appearance in 1970 of Charles E. Silberman's pivotal book *Crisis in the Classroom.* Interestingly enough, Silberman did not set out to write a book about educational reform. Rather, he undertook in 1966 a study of the education of educators under the auspices of the Carnegie Corporation of New York. The unwieldy phrase "education of educators" holds the clue to the initial intention of the study, namely, to go beyond traditional inquiries into the education of teachers, which had long concentrated on the role of schools and departments of education in preparing men and women for careers of service in the elementary and secondary schools, to a much broader inquiry into the role of universities in preparing responsible educators of the public.

"If our concern is with *education* . . . ," Silberman wrote in the prospectus for the study, "we cannot restrict our attention to the schools, for education is not synonymous with schooling. Children—and adults—learn outside school as

[10] Allen Graubard, "The Free School Movement," *Harvard Educational Review* 42 (1972): 351–73, and *Free the Children: Radical Reform and the Free School Movement* (New York: Pantheon Books, 1972). It is difficult to determine precisely whom to include as the key intellectuals of the later movement. John Holt included a bibliography in *Freedom and Beyond* (New York: E. P. Dutton, 1972); I also included one with "The Free School Movement: A Perspective," *Notes on Education,* no. 2 (October 1973). For an English analysis, see David H. Hargreaves, "De-schoolers and New Romantics," in Michael Flude and John Ahier, eds., *Educability, Schools and Ideology* (London: Croom Helm, 1974), pp. 186–210.

well as—perhaps more than—in school. To say this is not to denigrate the importance of the schools; it is to give proper weight to all the other educating forces in American society: the family and the community; student peer groups; television and the mass media; the armed forces; corporate training programs; libraries, museums, churches, boy scout troops, 4-H clubs. . . . Our concern in this study, therefore, is with the education of educators—journalists, television directors and producers, textbook publishers, and army generals as well as teachers (and college, junior college, and parochial school teachers as well as public school teachers)." [11]

Silberman insisted from the beginning, and wisely, that one could not make recommendations concerning the education of educators without some clear notion of what education itself would be like in the decades ahead. Hence, he projected as a major effort during the first phase of the study a survey of schools and other agencies of education, with a view to determining the fundamental directions of their development. The decision was auspicious, for, in a series of subtle shifts in purpose over the four years of the inquiry, the study gradually became an assessment of the educational reform movement of the 1960s that gathered and sorted the various strands of innovation and wove them into a coherent and persuasive program. Given the sponsorship of the Carnegie Corporation and the timeliness of Silberman's formulation, the book attracted widespread and respectful attention and did much to legitima-

[11] Charles E. Silberman, "The Carnegie Study of the Education of Educators: Preliminary Statement of Intent, September 26, 1966," unpublished memorandum, p. 2.

tize both the criticisms and the proposals of contemporary critics. And given Silberman's own intellectual sophistication—the study is surely the most learned and informed analysis to be associated with the recent reform movement—the book quickly became the most respected (though probably not the most widely read) theoretical statement of latter-day educational progressivism.

Silberman's analysis, therefore, is of special interest in tracing the fate of the Deweyan polarity concerning school and society; indeed, it exemplifies beautifully the continuing dilemma implicit in the Deweyan view. Silberman begins with an introduction that repeats the formulations of the prospectus: the concern of the book is with all the educating institutions—not only schools and colleges, but television, films, and the mass media, churches and synagogues, the law, medicine, and social work, museums and libraries, the armed forces, corporate training programs, and Boy Scout troops—and with the role of universities in preparing responsible professionals for service in these institutions. And Silberman's argument, stated early, is that the central problem with American education is not venality or indifference or stupidity, but mindlessness; hence, the solution lies in infusing the various educating institutions with purpose and, even more importantly, with thought about purpose and about the ways in which techniques, content, and organization fulfill or alter purpose. "We must find ways of stimulating educators— public school teachers, principals, and superintendents; college professors, deans, and presidents; radio, television, and film directors and producers; newspaper, magazine, and TV journalists and executives—to think about what they are doing, and why they are doing it. And we must persuade the general public to do the same." [12]

Thus far, Silberman's argument is quintessentially Deweyan. And so, thereafter, is the way in which the study proceeds. For, aside from a few brief remarks about the aridity of contemporary journalism, followed by the promise of another volume on the remaking of the less formal educating institutions, the remainder of the study deals wholly with schooling—including an indictment of its shortcomings, a series of proposals for its reform (much in the Deweyan mode), and a design for the kind of teacher education that will aid and abet that reform. At the end, in a brief afterword, Silberman assumes the characteristic Deweyan political posture. "To an extent characteristic of no other institution, save that of the state itself," Silberman quotes from Dewey, "the school has the power to modify the social order." Silberman then goes on to observe that "the crisis in the classroom is but one aspect of the larger crisis of American society as a whole, a crisis whose resolution is problematical at best. It does no good, however, to throw up our hands at the enormity of the task; we must take hold of it where we can, for the time for failure is long since past. We will not be able to create and maintain a humane society unless we create and maintain classrooms that are humane. But if we succeed in that endeavor—if we accomplish the remaking of American education—we will have gone a long way toward the larger task." Pending the arrival of the

[12] Charles E. Silberman, *Crisis in the Classroom: The Remaking of American Education* (New York: Random House, 1970), p. 11.

promised volume on the other educators, the school remains the principal lever for the creation and development of the good society.[13]

III

SILBERMAN was careful to distinguish in his study between his own views and those of the "romantic critics" such as John Holt, George Dennison, and Paul Goodman, much as Dewey before him had distinguished himself from partisans of the "child-centered" school. Later, however, the lines became blurred, as Silberman and the "romantic critics" exchanged endorsements of each other's views and writings at conferences and in the press. To Ivan Illich, however, they were all of a stripe. They were reformers, still committed to "the fundamental axioms of a schooled world." He alone was truly radical, for he alone understood that the most profound political issue facing the world was not how to improve schooling but whether to continue it at all.[14]

If Silberman's study burst upon the educational scene in 1970 with the full prestige of the Carnegie Corporation behind it, Ivan Illich's writings made their way with nothing more than the force of the author's charisma. Illich, a Roman Catholic priest caught up in the spirit of post-Johanine reformism, had founded the Center for International Documentation in

[13] Silberman, *Crisis in the Classroom*, pp. 522–24.
[14] Silberman, *Crisis in the Classroom*, pp. 209–10; Ivan Illich, *Deschooling Society* (New York: Harper & Row, 1971), p. 67.

Cuernavaca, Mexico, in an effort to stymie a large-scale missionary movement from North to South America that he thought would be deleterious to the Latin Americans. His studies at the Center and earlier as a parish priest in New York City's Spanish Harlem and as vice-rector of the Catholic University of Puerto Rico had led him to a radical rejection of all modern institutions—he referred to them as the "bureaucratic agencies of the corporate state," by which he meant the school, the consumer-family, the party, the army, the church, and the media of communication. And, in a series of pungent essays collected in three brief volumes, *Celebration of Awareness* (1970), *Deschooling Society* (1971), and *Tools for Conviviality* (1973), he developed the case for "the disestablishment of schooling" as a paradigmatic argument against the bureaucratic agencies he saw as ultimately destructive of the most essential human values.[15]

Unlike Silberman, Illich was scarcely indebted to Dewey; his arguments stemmed rather from the anti-institutionalism of the German theologian Dietrich Bonhoeffer. Yet Illich had a kinship with Dewey in his call for institutions of work, leisure, and politics that would ultimately be judged by their ability to foster human growth and learning. And his argument is significant at this point for the additional light it throws on the Deweyan dilemma, for Illich recognized as well as any educational theorist of the 1970s that many situations and institutions educate, of which the school is merely one. Yet Illich was prepared to stand the Deweyan solution on its head, contending that until people were freed of the modern

[15] Illich, *Deschooling Society*, p. 2.

16

curse of systematic schooling, education in the other institutions would be severely constrained. "School is not, by any means, the only modern institution which has as its primary purpose the shaping of man's vision of reality," Illich observed in *Deschooling Society*. "The hidden curriculum of family life, draft, health care, so-called professionalism, or of the media play an important part in the institutional manipulation of man's world-vision, language, and demands. But school enslaves more profoundly and more systematically, since only school is credited with the principal function of forming critical judgment, and, paradoxically, tries to do so by making learning about oneself, about others, and about nature depend on a prepackaged process. School touches us so intimately that none of us can expect to be liberated from it by something else." [16]

In place of schooling, as the quintessential (and universal) "manipulative" institution, Illich proposed the development of "convivial" educational institutions called learning webs—voluntary networks that would permit any student at any time to gain access to any educational resource that might help him define and achieve his own goals. Four such networks were proposed: Reference Services in Educational Objects, which would provide access to things or processes used for formal learning in such places as libraries, laboratories, museums, theatres, factories, farms, and airports (Richard Saul Wurnam's *Yellow Pages of Learning Resources* [1972] probably concretizes these reference services as well as any single source); Skill Exchanges, which would enable those who

[16] Illich, *Deschooling Society*, p. 47.

wished to learn certain skills to meet those willing to teach or model them; Peer Matching, which would permit informal voluntary association in the cause of learning; and Reference Services to Educators-at-Large, which would provide access to professionals, paraprofessionals, and free lances willing to teach under certain stipulated conditions. As a way of financing this apparatus, Illich suggested the creation of a publicly supported educational passport or "edu-credit" card, granted to each citizen at birth and carrying a lifelong entitlement to a certain amount of education. [17]

One might criticize Illich's analysis on several counts—the egregious caricature of the effects of schooling, the simplistic understanding of human nature (the more extraordinary, given Illich's theological sophistication), and the romantic vision of what would actually come to pass once people were left wholly to the mercy of popular huckstering and entertainment via the media. But for purposes of the argument here, neither criticisms nor further details are important. What is important is an understanding of education vis-à-vis the polity. In Illich's view, the polity for all intents and purposes absorbs the educative function and becomes the people in their convivial relationships, while, conversely, the people in their convivial relationships constitute the polity and in so doing educate one another. Actually, Illich achieves in theory the utopia Dewey sketched in 1933, of which the most utopian characteristic was that it had no schools, and children—nay, all people—learned what they needed to know in informal association with one another. The achievement—for all its grotesqueness—may

[17] Illich, *Deschooling Society*, pp. 78–79.

explain the enormous if momentary fascination of Illich's ideas for American intellectuals during the brief high noon of educational reform during the early 1970s.[18]

IV

DEWEY once forecast that the time would come when the progressive education movement would drop the term "progressive" and transform the debate over education into an argument over alternative views of the good life. It would then be clear, he observed, "that the real issue is between education which is genuinely educative and that which is in fact *mis*educative; and that the conflict between the old, the routine and mechanized, and the new, the living and moving, represents in fact the struggle to discover and put in practice the materials and methods which, under the conditions of present life, are truly educative." [19]

I suspect that Dewey's forecast has long since come to pass, and, indeed, I have argued elsewhere that by the 1950s the more fundamental tenets of the progressives had become the conventional wisdom of American education. The programs proposed in the several Conant reports, the innovations celebrated in Arthur D. Morse's *Schools of Tomorrow—Today*

---

[18] For a liberal critique of Illich's views, see Sidney Hook, "Illich's De-Schooled Utopia," *Encounter* 38 (1972): 53–57. For a radical critique, see Herbert Gintis, "Towards a Political Economy of Education: A Radical Critique of Ivan Illich's *Deschooling Society*," *Harvard Educational Review* 42 (1972): 70–96.

[19] John Dewey, "Introduction," in Agnes de Lima, *The Little Red School House* (New York: Macmillan, 1942), p. ix.

(1960), and the curriculum reforms that grew out of the work of the School Mathematics Study Group, the Physical Science Study Committee, and their counterparts in the other fields of knowledge did not reverse the main principles of progressivism but rather confirmed and extended them. In fact, the free-school movement of the sixties and even to an extent the de-schooling movement of the late 1960s and early 1970s (insofar as it connected with an earlier anarchist strain of thought within the progressive education movement) maintained an essentially continuous tradition of pedagogical protest and reform. Yet the very fact of that continuity makes the dilemma of the progressives burningly contemporary and insistently our own.[20]

Dewey feared toward the end of his life that the achievements of the progressive era would be nullified by efforts "to turn the clock back in education." He was even more concerned, however, lest the progressive education movement itself ossify into a series of fixed principles, standard procedures,

[20] I argued the case for seeing the curriculum reform movement of the 1950s and early 1960s as essentially continuous with the earlier progressive education movement in *The Genius of American Education* (Pittsburgh: University of Pittsburgh Press, 1965), pp. 54–55. On the other hand, I failed to give proper attention to the anarchist strain of thought in the earlier movement in *The Transformation of the School: Progressivism in American Education, 1876–1957* (New York: Alfred A. Knopf, 1961). For a good account of that strain, see Laurence Veysey, *The Communal Experience: Anarchist and Counter-Cultures in America* (New York: Harper & Row, 1973), chap. 2. It is worth noting that those who attempted to articulate an anarchist philosophy of education, notably Elizabeth Byrne Ferm and Alexis C. Ferm, were themselves committed to schooling and actually conducted schools. The Ferms were associated for some years with The Modern School at Stelton, New Jersey, which was named after the Escuela Moderna of the noted Spanish anarchist Francisco Ferrer. See Elizabeth Byrne Ferm, *Freedom in Education* (New York: Lear Publishers, 1949), and Arthur Mark, "Two Libertarian Educators: Elizabeth Byrne Ferm and Alexis Constantine Ferm (1857–1971)" (doctoral dissertation, Teachers College, Columbia University, 1974).

and ready-made rules, trotted out like mustard plasters as external remedies for basic problems. "It should be a commonplace," Dewey remarked in his last published essay on education, "but unfortunately it is not, that no education—or anything else for that matter—is progressive unless it is making progress. Nothing is more reactionary in its consequences than the effort to live according to the ideas, principles, customs, habits, or institutions which at some time in the past represented a change for the better but which in the present constitute factors in the problems confronting us. . . . New problems demand for their intelligent solution the projection of new purposes, new ends in view; and new ends necessitate the development of new means and methods." And all of these, one might add, demand new definitions of the problems to be solved and of the elements that must figure in their solution.[21]

Let us return, then, to the formulations of *Democracy and Education* in an effort toward redefinition. The place where Dewey went awry, it appears, is the point in his discussion of incidental versus intentional education where he dwelled on the origins of institutions rather than their functions. What matter that the family may have *begun* in the desire to gratify appetites and secure the perpetuation of a line? What matter that religious associations may have *begun* in the desire to ward off evil influences and secure the favor of supreme powers? What matter that organized work may have *begun* in enslavement to others? For one thing, we can't really know how they began; for another, the question of origins may not be central to the argument. The important fact is that family life

[21] John Dewey, "Introduction," in Elsie Ripley Clapp, *The Use of Resources in Education* (New York: Harper & Brothers, 1952), pp. viii, ix.

does educate, religious life does educate, and organized work does educate; and, what is more, the education of all three realms is as intentional as the education of the school, however different in kind and quality.

Every family has a curriculum, which it teaches quite deliberately and systematically over time. Every church and synagogue has a curriculum, which it teaches deliberately and systematically over time—the Old and New Testaments, after all, are among our oldest curricula, and so are the Missal and the Mass, and so is the Book of Common Prayer. And every employer has a curriculum, which he teaches deliberately and systematically over time; the curriculum includes not only the technical skills of typing or welding or reaping or teaching but also the social skills of carrying out those activities in concert with others on given time schedules and according to established expectations and routines. One can go on to point out that libraries have curricula, museums have curricula, Boy Scout troops have curricula, and day-care centers have curricula, and most important, perhaps, radio and television stations have curricula—and by these curricula I refer not only to programs labeled educational but also to news broadcasts and documentaries (which presumably inform), to commercials (which teach people to want), and to soap operas (which reinforce common myths and values).[22]

[22] On familial education, see Hope Jensen Leichter, ed., *The Family as Educator* (New York: Teachers College Press, 1975). There is an immense literature of homiletics, or the art of preaching, which is revealing of the church or synagogue as educator in its own right (as contrasted with the literature of "religious education," which tends to deal more limitedly with classroom instruction under church or synagogue auspices). On the factory as educator in the sense in which I am using the term, see Alex Inkeles and David H. Smith, *Becoming Modern: Individual Change in Six Developing Countries* (Cambridge, Mass.: Harvard University Press, 1974), especially chap. 10,

Some Problems in the Progressive Theory of Education

To specify this range of institutions is to extricate us from the Deweyan polarity of all life being broadly educative and overwhelmingly powerful and the school being intentionally educative but not very powerful at all. Rather, we have a theory of education whereby each of the major educative agencies performs a mediative role with respect to the others and with respect to society at large. The family mediates the culture, and it also mediates the ways in which religious organizations, television broadcasters, schools, and employers mediate the culture. Families not only teach in their own right, they also screen and interpret the teaching of churches, synagogues, television broadcasters, schools, and employers. One could go on and work out all the permutations and combinations. What is more, these various institutions mediate the culture in a variety of pedagogical modes and through a range of technologies for the recording, sharing, and distributing of symbols. In effect, they define the terms of effective participation and growth in the society.[23]

Remaining within the broad Deweyan context, we can posit

---

entitled "The Factory as a School in Modernity." On television as educator, see Herbert J. Gans, "The Mass Media as an Educational Institution," *Television Quarterly* 6 (Spring 1967): 20–37; the several essays in Richard Adler, ed., *Television as a Social Force: New Approaches to TV Criticism* (New York: Praeger, 1975), especially Douglass Cater, "Television and Thinking People," and Paul H. Weaver, "Newspaper News and Television News"; *Television and Growing Up: The Impact of Televised Violence*, Report to the Surgeon General, United States Public Health Service, Department of Health, Education and Welfare, 1971; Robert M. Liebert, John M. Neale, and Emily S. Davidson, *The Early Window: Effects of Television on Children and Youth* (New York: Pergamon Press, 1973); and Gerald S. Lesser, *Children and Television: Lessons from Sesame Street* (New York: Random House, 1974).

[23] I am using *mediate* here as a generic term for a variety of functions, including screening, interpreting, criticizing, reinforcing, complementing, counteracting, and transforming. See Hope Jensen Leichter, "Some Perspectives on the Family as Educator," *Teachers College Record* 76 (1974–75): 213–15.

a new formulation: the theory of education is the theory of the relation of various educative interactions and institutions to one another and to the society at large. And within such a theory the Deweyan dilemma dissolves, as the interactions between education and the polity become more diverse and the opportunities for public influence thereby more numerous and accessible.[24]

[24] The commonsense use of the concept *society* as a means of referring to the broader context in which particular social activities take place is admittedly problematical but nevertheless helpful (Leon H. Mayhew discusses the issues in the article on "Society" in the *International Encyclopedia of the Social Sciences*, David L. Sills, ed., 17 vols. [New York: Macmillan and the Free Press, 1968], 14: 578). My intention is to allude to the political, economic, and social institutions to which educative institutions inevitably relate, though I am well aware that, given my definition of education, political, economic, and social institutions are themselves in some respects educative.

TOWARD AN ECOLOGY

OF EDUCATION

———

I HAVE FOUND IT fruitful to define education as the deliberate, systematic, and sustained effort to transmit, evoke, or acquire knowledge, attitudes, values, skills, or sensibilities, as well as any outcomes of that effort. The definition stresses intentionality, though I am well aware that learning takes place in many situations where intentionality is not present. It makes room for study as well as instruction, thereby embracing the crucial realm of self-education. And it acknowledges that behavior, preferences, and tastes are involved, as well as knowledge and understanding. It sees education as a process more limited than what the sociologist would call socialization or the anthropologist enculturation, though obviously inclusive of many of the same phenomena. And it recognizes that there is often conflict between what educators are trying to teach and what is learned from the ordinary business of living.[1]

The definition is latitudinarian, in that it permits us several angles of vision with respect to the interplay of generations. Education may be viewed as intergenerational, with adults teaching children (the historian Bernard Bailyn once defined education as "the entire process by which culture transmits itself across the generations") or with children teaching adults (one thinks of immigrant families in which children, having learned the new culture relatively rapidly, become its interpreters to parents and grandparents); it may be viewed as intragenerational (recall Robert F. Berkhofer's account of Protestant missions to the American Indians in *Salvation and the Savage* [1965], which makes such apt use of the concept of acculturation); or it may be viewed as a self-conscious coming of age (so often the leitmotif of the reflective memoir or autobiography).[2]

[1] The substance of this essay appeared initially as "Notes Toward a Theory of Education," *Notes on Education*, no. 1 (June 1973): 4–6, and "Further Notes Toward a Theory of Education," *Notes on Education*, no. 4 (March 1974): 1–6. For the numerous current definitions and interpretations of socialization, see David A. Goslin, ed., *Handbook of Socialization Theory and Research* (Chicago: Rand McNally, 1969). For similar perspectives on enculturation, see John J. Honigmann, ed., *Handbook of Social and Cultural Anthropology* (Chicago: Rand McNally, 1973), chap. 25, and Francis L. K. Hsu, ed., *Psychological Anthropology*, new ed. (Cambridge, Mass.: Schenckman, 1972).

[2] Bernard Bailyn, *Education in the Forming of American Society* (Chapel Hill: University of North Carolina Press, 1960), p. 14. The educational tension in the immigrant family is portrayed in Oscar Handlin, *The Uprooted* (Boston: Little, Brown, 1951), chap. 9. Margaret Mead uses the concept of the "immigrant in time" to dramatize the extent to which modern children, who are more adaptable to changing conditions than their parents and grandparents, end up having to interpret novelty to their parents and grandparents. See *Culture and Commitment: A Study of the Generation Gap* (New York: The Natural History Press, 1970), chap. 3.

The definition also projects us beyond the schools and colleges to the multiplicity of individuals and institutions that educate—parents, peers, siblings, and friends, as well as families, churches, synagogues, libraries, museums, summer camps, benevolent societies, agricultural fairs, settlement houses, factories, radio stations, and television networks. It alerts us to the numerous occupational groups (only some of which have been professionalized) associated with educational institutions and to the variety of pedagogies they employ. And it suggests the fact that each of these pedagogies tends at a given time to impinge on the others. Thus, revivalist preaching doubtless influenced familial instruction in the nineteenth century, while *Sesame Street* unquestionably influences kindergarten instruction in our own.

Finally, the definition grants that education ordinarily (though not necessarily) produces outcomes, some of which may be intended and some unintended, and indeed that the unintended outcomes may be more significant than the intended. It also grants that other phenomena, from politics to commerce to technology to earthquakes, may produce even more significant changes in understanding, behavior, or sensibility than education. There are some who would consider all such phenomena educative, for they invariably shape human beings and affect their destinies. I find their definition so inclusive as to be meaningless. We obviously learn many things that no one sets out to teach us and that we ourselves do not set out to learn. No one interested in education can afford to ignore such incidental learning, but to call it education is to blur and confuse that critical realm of human activity in which individuals seek purposefully and planfully to bring about changes in their own or others' thinking, behavior, or sensibilities.

Every day in every part of the world people set out to teach something to others or to study something themselves (or to place others or themselves in situations from which they hope desirable changes in knowledge, attitudes, skills, or appreciations will result). They deserve a theory specifically addressed to their problems and purposes, one that will assist them to act more intelligently, ever hopeful of the possibilities but fully aware of the limitations and risks that attend their efforts.

II

GIVEN an awareness of the multiplicity of institutions that educate, one soon perceives the tendency of such institutions at particular times and places to relate to one another in what might be called configurations of education. Each of the institutions within a configuration interacts with the others and with the larger society that sustains it and that is in turn affected by it. Configurations of education also interact, as configurations, with the society of which they are part.

Relationships among the institutions that constitute a configuration of education may be political, pedagogical, or personal. There may be overlapping lines of support and control—one thinks of the hold of Protestant missionary organizations on the families, churches, and schools of Ohio Valley towns during the nineteenth century, or of the interlocking influence of a genteel upper class on the museums, libraries, and scientific societies of eastern seaboard cities during the twentieth. Or there may be substantial pedagogical influence extending from one institution to another within the configuration—consider, for example, the spread of entertainment styles from cinema and television to churches, colleges, and adult education organizations during our own time. Or, indeed, there may be decisive personal influence deriving from the same people moving as teachers or students through more than one institution—such has always been the case with the configurations of education maintained by small sectarian communities like the Mennonites, the Hasidic Jews, and the Black Muslims.

The relationships among the institutions constituting a configuration of education may be complementary or contradictory, consonant or dissonant. Thus, for example, church and school may be subject to similar sources of control but may end up competing vigorously for funds and programs—one perceives the problem in the effort of present-day Roman Catholic theorists (and budgeters) to distinguish pastoral from educative functions in working out policies regarding parochial schools. Or they may operate in a near-perfect complementarity in which the church deals with values and the school deals with knowledge and each recognizes the role of the other—such was often the case with the Protestant church and the public school in the small towns of trans-Allegheny America during the nineteenth and early twentieth centuries (one need only compare the publications of the American Tract Society with the McGuffey readers).

Or, to take another example, family and school may share a mutual concern for the child's intellectual development, but the teacher may be more demanding at the same time as the parent is more sustaining—the tension is at the heart of William Gibson's lovely drama *The Miracle Worker* (1960), about the education of Helen Keller. Or the teacher may attempt to liberate (by proffering intellectual, moral, or vocational alternatives) at the same time as the parent attempts to constrain— one thinks of countless instances in which parents prefer the immediate earnings of a dependent child to the continuance of a school career that would defer earnings but almost certainly increase them once independence was achieved. Or, bearing in mind Jerome Bruner's distinction between enactive, ikonic, and symbolic learning, the family may emphasize enactive and ikonic education (particularly as it mediates television education), while the school emphasizes symbolic education.[3]

However these relationships develop, they must be ascertained in their particularity rather than assumed in some kind of generality. Institutions do manifest a certain stubborn persistence with respect to their roles and functions, and it is only reasonable to anticipate that families will be concerned with the values of their children, that schools will attempt to stimulate cognitive development, and that libraries will encourage the use of books. Yet there is all too frequently an unexpected

[3] Jerome S. Bruner, *The Relevance of Education* (New York: W. W. Norton, 1971), pp. 7–8, 18. See also David R. Olson, *Cognitive Development: The Child's Acquisition of Diagonality* (New York: Academic Press, 1970), pp. 193–97, and David R. Olson, ed., *Media and Symbols: The Forms of Expression, Communication, and Education* (Chicago: University of Chicago Press, 1974), chaps. 1 and 6.

gap between what ought to be, logically, and what is, actually: parents have been known to abandon their children; schools have often failed to honor intellect; and there are libraries more interested in possessing books than permitting people to read them.

There is obviously an inescapable relationship between the concept of the configuration of education and the concept of the community. Most utopian writers have recognized this, depicting their utopias as perfect configurations of education in which all the constituent agencies and institutions are consonant and complementary in their efforts and effects—a fact, incidentally, that makes Dewey's 1933 utopia all the more interesting. In real communities, however, such consonance and complementarity are usually obviated by the presence of alternative configurations of education and by the fact that individual educational institutions are often mediating external (and conflicting) influences.

The American experience is illuminating in this respect. In my own studies of the colonies, I found it fruitful to consider the multiple and changing relationships between families, churches, and schools (and, where present, colleges and printing presses) in a New England town (Dedham, Massachusetts), a southern county (Elizabeth City, Virginia), and two middle-colony market towns (Philadelphia and New York) as paradigmatic colonial configurations of education. For all the characteristic simplicity and localism of the era, and despite efforts in New England actually to construct a utopia, any congruence between configuration and community was at best partial. During the seventeenth century, all four communities were in continuing communication with the cultural centers of Great Britain and Continental Europe: families studied a didactic literature prepared and printed in London and Edinburgh; churches and schools employed pedagogical styles that derived variously from France, Switzerland, and the Dutch Republic; and amateur scientists exchanged data with their counterparts in a dozen European cities. The point is not to deny the significance of the local and indigenous; it is merely to argue that, even in the earliest phases of colonial development, educational institutions were already mediating diverse external influences and communities were not simply isolated geographical localities. By the eighteenth century all four communities had developed multiple configurations of education that only partially overlapped: one could live one's earliest years amid a cluster of white families in a Dedham neighborhood dominated by a New Light or Old Light pastor and only later enter into any kind of enduring association with other sorts of children and adults in a district school; one could spend one's childhood amid a cluster of black families in a New York neighborhood and only later enter into what was at best a set of sharply restricted relationships with white families of any kind.[4]

By the nineteenth century most local communities embraced multiple configurations of education and most configurations of education comprised institutions that were increasingly mediating nonlocal influences. Families in Indiana read books printed in New England hawked by colporteurs based in

[4] Lawrence A. Cremin, *American Education: The Colonial Experience, 1607–1783* (New York: Harper & Row, 1970), chaps. 8 and 17.

Cincinnati; churches and Sunday schools in Tennessee taught liturgies and disciplines developed in Europe and enforced by itinerant or absent diocesan authorities; quarter-communities on Virginia plantations were in touch with liberation movements in the North and in the West Indies; and newspapers in New York printed material transmitted by cable and telegraph from the far corners of the earth. In the twentieth century, the evolution of new educational institutions and the emergence of metropolitan and transnational communities (facilitated by the revolution in communications, notably network television) accelerated both developments, ultimately transforming the very nature of the local and the cosmopolitan. Today Americans are confronted with a more bewildering variety of configurations of education than ever, yet they are subject to a greater commonality of educational influences.

There is a final point to be made, about the relation of configurations of education to the phenomena of social stability and change. Inasmuch as educational institutions and configurations transmit culture to the young, they have played a time-honored role in maintaining social stability and continuity, though it is important to note that cultural conflict and confusion can be transmitted quite as effectively as cultural consonance and coherence (one need only examine the Lynds' chapter on the Middletown spirit in their classic studies of Muncie, Indiana, to be aware of the problem as it confronted Muncie's families, schools, and churches during the 1920s and 1930s). Moreover, educational institutions and configurations have also played an important role in stimulating and accelerating social change—one thinks of the impact of radical pastors and printers during the era of the American Revolution or of the impact of television news (and commercials) on some of the leading social movements of our own time.[5]

With respect to such phenomena, an ecological approach to education, one that views educational institutions and configurations in relation to one another and to the larger society that sustains them and is in turn affected by them, can prove instructive. Thus, for example, what we have traditionally thought of as the extraordinary influence of the nineteenth-century common school (especially in small-town America west of the Alleghenies, where it reached a kind of apotheosis) derived not so much from the common school per se as from a configuration of education of which the common school was only one element. Ordinarily including the white Protestant family, the white Protestant church, and the white Protestant Sunday school along with the common school, it was a configuration in which the values and pedagogies of the several component institutions happened to be mutually supportive. Other contemporary configurations were fraught with internal conflict. Thus, if one considers the Indian reservation as a configuration of education, one is immediately impressed by the tensions between familial instruction and missionary instruction, between Indian values and white values, between the virtues of resistance and the virtues of accommodation.[6]

In sum, when seeking the sources of social stability and

[5] Robert S. Lynd and Helen Merrell Lynd, *Middletown in Transition: A Study in Cultural Conflicts* (New York: Harcourt, Brace, 1937), chap. 12.

[6] The concept of ecology is useful because of its stress on relationships, though it carries with it a certain metaphysical freight from biology that is not relevant here.

change (and especially of social reform and resistance to reform), one must consider the possible contributions of all the institutions that educate, bearing in mind that the decisive elements may still lie elsewhere. The precise balance, among educational institutions and between education and other factors, will vary from one historical circumstance to another, so that no easy generalizations—Marxian or otherwise—will suffice. At the very least, however, one will avoid claiming too much for education (even in the more comprehensive sense suggested here).

One final point is worthy of note. At any given time a society will tend to rely on one or another of the agencies of education as the critical instrument of deliberate nurture: Americans turned most often to the family and the church in the seventeenth and eighteenth centuries, and to the school in the nineteenth and twentieth. The institutions chosen may not be the most powerful or even the most effective; yet the very fact that they are chosen may enhance their influence, both within the configuration of which they are part and on the society they seek to affect.

III

INDIVIDUALS come to educational situations with their own temperaments, histories, and purposes, and different individuals will obviously interact with a given configuration of education in different ways and with different outcomes. Hence, in considering the interactions and the outcomes, it is as necessary to examine individual life histories as it is to examine the configurations themselves. An educational life history focuses on the experience of education from the perspective of the person having and undergoing the experience (the anthropologist would say, from the "ego perspective")—the experience resulting from the deliberate, systematic, and sustained efforts of others to transmit or evoke knowledge, attitudes, values, skills, and sensibilities, as well as the experience involved in the person's own deliberate, systematic, and sustained efforts to acquire knowledge, attitudes, values, skills, and sensibilities.[7]

An educational life history will ordinarily begin with the efforts of others (parents, kin, peers, clergymen, schoolteachers) to nurture certain attitudes and behaviors and to teach certain knowledge and values, and with the individual's response to these efforts, which leads on the one hand to selective accommodations and patterns of believing, knowing, and doing, and on the other hand to an inevitable impact on those undertaking the nurturing and teaching. From the perspective of education, a key phenomenon in the process is the emergence of a characteristic life-style in the maturing individual, the core of which might be described using Gordon W. Allport's concept of the "proprium." One behavioral characteristic of a maturing individual is an increasing measure of propriate striving, part of which clearly takes the form of intentional efforts to develop the self along particular lines, or, alternatively, efforts at

[7] The most comprehensive recent review of the substantial literature on life histories in the social sciences is L. L. Langness, *The Life History in Anthropological Science* (New York: Holt, Rinehart and Winston, 1965).

self-education. In the Socratic sense, propriate striving is to the individual what *paideia* is to the society; the former conceives of education as individual aspiration, the latter, as social aspiration. Both are products of the examined life. Granted this, one must be wary of portraying educational development as any simple, direct, or linear progression from mere responsiveness to propriate striving, or of assuming that in the absence of propriate striving there is no educational development, or of supposing that only intellectuals examine their lives. And one must always bear in mind that many factors other than education play a role in the making of individuality.[8]

One key element in any educational life history is the emergence of what my colleague Hope Jensen Leichter has referred to as an educative style, a set of characteristic ways in which an individual engages in, moves through, and combines educational experiences over a lifetime. Presumably, she argues, these modes begin to be learned in early encounters with "educationally significant others," and are then rein-

[8] Gordon W. Allport, *Becoming: Basic Considerations for a Psychology of Personality* (New York: Holt, Rinehart and Winston, 1965), pp. 45–51. The term *paideia* as used here and elsewhere in these essays is especially valuable because of the several meanings it incorporates. The ancient Greeks used it variously and often interchangeably to mean "education," "culture," or "social, political, or ethical aspiration." I am using it in this instance primarily in the last sense. Given the social emphasis in these various meanings, there have been those who have considered the concept of *paideia* incompatible with individual freedom and growth; it might be well for them to recall that the same ancient Greeks employed the term *politeuesthai* as meaning both "to live" and "to take part in communal life." For them, as for John Dewey two thousand years later, individuality was impossible to define apart from some version of community life. See Werner Jaeger, *Paideia: The Ideals of Greek Culture*, trans. Gilbert Highet, 3 vols. (New York: Oxford University Press, 1939–44), 1: 110 and *passim*.

forced or modified, confirmed or disconfirmed, in subsequent experience. They become, in their totality, the pattern according to which an individual approaches, undergoes, pursues, and organizes education. Benjamin Franklin lived his whole life as a series of educational projects whereby he constantly tried to shape and reshape his character and sensibilities—at least that is how he preferred to characterize his life in the *Autobiography*. Frederick Douglass reminisced about the ways in which, as a youngster, he systematically used his friendships with white age-mates as opportunities for learning to read. And Margaret Sanger appears to have imbibed a fierce and courageous independence from her father, which then marked all her subsequent approaches to education (and everything else). Educative style is itself subject to continued testing and change over a lifetime; yet it does provide an important element of continuity as an individual moves from one institution to another within a configuration and from one configuration to another. Furthermore, while educative style will generally come to include propriate striving as an individual matures, educative style is the broader and more comprehensive phenomenon, comprising many other components.[9]

An individual with a discernible educative style and a measure of educative autonomy will approach a particular educational institution or configuration of institutions with his own purposes, his own agenda, and his own habits of learning. The result will surely be a unique interaction, the outcome of which cannot be predicted by looking at either the institu-

[9] Hope Jensen Leichter, "The Concept of Educative Style," *Teachers College Record* 75 (1973–74): 239–250.

tion(s) or the individual in isolation. Moreover, by intent or happenstance, an individual will develop his own network of "educationally significant others," which may or may not correspond to any established configuration of education. The son of a religiously orthodox family will defy parents, peers, and clergymen to attend a secular college; the daughter of an insistently skeptical family will turn her back on parents, peers, and teachers to join a fundamentalist commune; a youngster of uncertain goals and aspirations will happen upon a particular adult and for his own reasons choose that adult as exemplar and teacher. The cases are legion; the point is to distinguish between the external relationships involved in the patterning of educational institutions and the particular experience of individuals.

One of the most difficult problems in studying educational life histories is to differentiate among maturation, learning, development, and education. Using rough definitions, maturation refers to changes in an individual that are relatively independent of external conditions or experience; learning refers to changes in behavior that result from experience; and development refers to changes in an individual that result from the interaction of maturation and learning. Education as here defined is obviously different from development, though closely related to it. From the perspective of the individual, education refers to his or her own deliberate efforts to acquire knowledge, attitudes, values, skills, and sensibilities, as well as to any outcomes of those efforts; and it refers also to the outcomes of such efforts by others. In much the same way that education ideally results in learning though all learning is not necessarily a result of education, so education ideally contributes to development though all development is not necessarily a result of education.[10]

An educational biography is an account or portrayal of an individual life, focusing on the experience of education. There is an obvious relationship between the concept of educational biography and the more general concept of biography itself. In fact, given a sufficiently broad definition of education and a subject with a sufficiently well-defined proprium, the two concepts merge. They have also merged in a number of classic autobiographies, notably Benjamin Franklin's, John Stuart Mill's, and Henry Adams's. In this respect, James Olney's notion of the "metaphors of self," put forward in his recently published theory of autobiography, is fruitful. Metaphors, Olney argues, "are something known and of our making, or at least of our choosing, that we put to stand for, and so to help us understand, something unknown and not of our making; they are that by which the lonely subjective consciousness gives order not only to itself but to as much of the objective reality as it is capable of formalizing and of controlling." It is important to recognize that such metaphors as they appear in autobiographies are ordinarily retrospective and hence far more clear, simple, and certain than what Olney

[10] For the numerous current definitions and interpretations of development, see L. R. Goulet and Paul B. Bates, eds., *Life-Span Developmental Psychology: Research and Theory* (New York: Academic Press, 1970), and Paul B. Bates and K. Warner Schaie, eds., *Life-Span Developmental Psychology: Personality and Socialization* (New York: Academic Press, 1973). See also Lawrence Kohlberg and Rochelle Mayer, "Development as the Aim of Education," *Harvard Educational Review* 42 (1972): 449–96. Kohlberg and Mayer claim to put forward a synthesis of the Deweyan and Piagetian psychologies, but the outcome strikes me as more Piagetian than Deweyan.

refers to as the "objective reality" of the life. Moreover, every-one has some kind of metaphor of self, even in the absence of a written autobiography and even though the metaphor may be conceived and expressed in commonsense terms. Follow-ing Olney's formulation, an educational biographer might ask: What "metaphors of self" did the subject seem to choose or come to believe? How did these metaphors influence the sub-ject's quest for education and response to it? And how in turn were the metaphors confirmed or modified by education? [11]

IV

IN ITS MOST general sense, the process of education is on the one hand a series of transactions between an individual with a particular temperament and life history and one or more institutions of education that tend to relate to one an-other in configurations, and on the other hand a series of de-liberate efforts toward self-development. It is a complex pro-cess, fraught with irony and contradiction. The teacher and the taught often differ in educational aim and outlook, as do both in many instances from the sponsor. What is taught is not always what is desired, and vice versa. What is taught is not always what is learned, and vice versa. And when what is taught is actually learned, it is frequently learned over lengthy periods of time and at the once, twice, and thrice removed, so that the intended and the incidental end up merging in such a

[11] James Olney, *Metaphors of Self: The Meaning of Autobiography* (Princeton: Princeton University Press, 1972), p. 30.

way as to become virtually indistinguishable. Moreover, there are almost always unintended consequences in education; indeed, they are often more significant than those that are intended.

Beyond this, there is always a great deal going on in any educational transaction, and at many levels. The late Jules Henry once referred to learning as "polyphasic," by which he meant that human beings have a strong innate tendency to learn more than one thing at a time. The term might be applied to teaching as well. Multiple intentions are almost always involved in education and multiple outcomes are almost always the result. Furthermore, both the intentions and the outcomes are as often contradictory as they are complementary. Education never liberates without at the same time limiting, and it never empowers without at the same time constraining. Hence, the problem is rarely one of total freedom versus total control but rather what the balance is, and to what end, and in light of what alternatives. Finally, it is almost a truism that the outcomes of education are seldom simultaneous and frequently delayed, and that the overall effect of any particular effort cannot be ascertained, so to speak, until all the results are in.[12]

There has been a marked tendency in recent years to conceive of educational transactions simplistically, using com-

[12] Jules Henry, "Culture, Education, and Communications Theory," in George D. Spindler, ed., *Education and Anthropology* (Stanford: Stanford University Press, 1955), pp. 196–99. See also Henry's remarkable "A Cross-Cultural Outline of Education," which suggests many of the propositions proffered here, in *Jules Henry on Education* (New York: Random House, 1971), pp. 72–183.

monsense assumptions from everyday life or borrowing isolated theories from one or another of the behavioral sciences.
There is a good deal of popular commentary, for example, that
conceives of the school as the sole educator and the student as
some kind of tabula rasa, and then goes on to imply that
schoolbooks embody the essence of schooling, so that once the
content of the schoolbooks has been ascertained the effects of
schooling can be deduced. Assumptions such as these dominated the bitter controversies over education that rent Kanawha County, West Virginia, during 1974 and 1975.[13]

In quite different fashion a number of recent historians have
attempted to draw upon modern behavioral science theories in
developing a more sophisticated understanding of educational
transactions, but the theories have too often been imperfectly
applied or applied without adequate reference to data, leading
to what are at best truncated versions of the educational process. Thus, for example, Stanley Elkins, in his pioneering
study of *Slavery* (1959), applied Bruno Bettelheim's psychoan-

[13] I am indebted for the notion of commonsense analysis to Fritz Heider, *The Psychology of Interpersonal Relations* (New York: John Wiley, 1958), chap. 4. The point
is worth noting that commonsense analysis is not necessarily simple and often quite
the opposite. Indeed, a number of scholars have taken commonsense knowledge,
thinking, and decision making as topics for systematic investigation. See, for example,
Harold Garfinkel, *Studies in Ethnomethodology* (Englewood Cliffs, N.J.: Prentice-
Hall, 1967), chaps. 2 and 3 and *passim*. One of the issues in the new ethnomethodology is the relation or resemblance—if any—between commonsense
thinking and scientific thinking (see, for example, the several reviews of the Garfinkel
volume in the *American Sociological Review* 33 [1968]: 122–30; Kenneth E. Bould-
ing, *The Image* [Ann Arbor: University of Michigan Press, 1956]; and John Dewey,
"Common Sense and Science: Their Respective Frames of Reference," *The Journal of
Philosophy* 45 [1948]: 197–208). My own analysis of the controversy in Kanawha
County, West Virginia, appeared in *The 1975 World Book Year Book* (Chicago: Field
Enterprises Educational Corporation, 1975), pp. 41–45.

alytical interpretations of concentration camp life under the Nazis in an effort to understand the development of the American slave personality during the ante-bellum period, and concluded that the same psychological mechanism that led concentration camp inmates to see themselves as their captors saw them led nineteenth-century slaves to manifest the childlike behavior represented by the Sambo stereotype. The difficulty with Elkins's analysis, however, is that it drew imperfectly on Bettelheim, focusing on only one of the several psychological mechanisms Bettelheim saw operative in the camps, and then went on to assert the applicability of that mechanism without reference to the evidence in the slave sources.[14]

Similarly, Michael Katz, in the imaginative essays he published as *Class, Bureaucracy, and Schools* (1971), relied heavily on the body of social theory addressed to the phenomenon of bureaucracy, a body of theory from which he inferred that the basic structure of an educational situation is a more powerful determinant of educational processes and outcomes than any curriculum the teachers themselves might choose to introduce. The theory of bureaucracy is obviously relevant to education—the structure of an institution will surely influence the ways in which it carries out its functions. But what Katz did was to trace the bureaucratization of urban schooling in the nineteenth century, assert that bureaucracy in the modern world had been a bourgeois invention representing "a crystallization of bourgeois social attitudes," and then infer that the decisive element in public school education over the past

---

[14] For the debate over Elkins's study, see Ann J. Lane, ed., *The Debate over Slavery: Stanley Elkins and His Critics* (Urbana: University of Illinois Press, 1971).

hundred years had been, pure and simple, an experience in planned social inequality whereby the bourgeoisie had exerted its control over the working class. Once again, the inference was made without reference to data concerning the educative experience itself.[15]

The tendency to conceive of educational transactions simplistically has also been manifest in recent discussions of educational theory (and policy) growing out of James S. Coleman's report on *Equality of Educational Opportunity* (1966). Coleman's data did indeed suggest that the effects of schooling were less potent and less uniform than had traditionally been assumed. His data did not indicate, however, that the school had no power, but rather that it was educating sequentially and synchronically along with other institutions and that its effect on different individuals was partly dependent on what happened to them in those other institutions. It is not that schooling lacks potency; it is rather that the potency of schooling must be seen in relation to the potency of other experience (some of which is educational in character) that has occurred earlier and is occurring elsewhere. The point has obvious bearing on assessments of the effects of schooling that ignore other educational factors, fail to hold them constant, or refuse to correct for them.

Presumably, it is theories of teaching and learning that will be at the heart of the effort to illumine the nature of educational transactions; yet it is abundantly clear that acculturation theories, role theories, and theories of human development

[15] Michael B. Katz, *Class, Bureaucracy, and Schools: The Illusion of Educational Change in America* (New York: Praeger, 1971), p. xxiii.

(including psychoanalytical theories) hold immense promise, as do a host of other theories stemming from the several behavioral disciplines that would seem at first glance only marginally relevant to education. Such theories are fruitful inasmuch as they point to the possible significance of certain educational data and offer possible explanations of certain educational phenomena, and they must be exploited to the fullest by those seeking insight into the processes of education. So also, of course, must the several scientific methods associated with the behavioral disciplines, from clinical observation to large-scale surveying, from physiological analysis to network charting.[16]

Granted this, the strictures John Dewey advanced almost a half-century ago in *The Sources of a Science of Education* (1929) remain as pertinent as ever—and they apply, incidentally, to the entire range of educational phenomena, configurations and life histories as well as transactions. However much educational scholarship must draw upon a wide variety of disciplines in the effort to illumine educational phenomena, it must remain alert to the inevitable partiality of the insights to be derived from any particular science and aware that in the last analysis it is the educational situation itself that must provide the subject matter to be studied and the arena in which the results of such study are tested and applied. "The sources of educational science," Dewey observed, "are any portions of ascertained knowledge that enter into the heart,

[16] Many of the relevant methods are ably discussed in Gardner Lindzey and Elliot Aronson, eds., *The Handbook of Social Psychology*, 2d ed., 5 vols. (Reading, Mass.: Addison-Wesley, 1968), vol. 2.

head and hands of educators, and which, by entering in, render the performance of the educational function more enlightened, more humane, more truly educational than it was before. But there is no way to discover what is 'more truly educational' except by the continuation of the educational act itself. The discovery is never made; it is always making." [17]

Two concluding observations are in order. First, though the thrust of the argument here is latitudinarian, nothing is meant to preclude the step-by-step systematic investigation of precisely defined problems that is the essence of scientific inquiry. The recognition that education is a complex phenomenon that goes on in many situations and institutions does not imply that every investigator must study everything all the time. What it does imply is that investigators must be alert to the complexity and range of education as they define their problems. The goal is not less definition but rather better definition in respect to the boundaries of problems and the particular phenomena deemed relevant and significant.

Finally, it is well to bear in mind that ideas, ideals, and values are always involved in education. They suggest certain images of human nature, of what is possible and desirable, and of how, when, and where to intervene (or not to intervene) to nurture what is possible and desirable. They alert both teacher and student to particular human potentialities and at the same time blind them to others. And they propel individuals to act—indeed, the most meaningful intellectual histories are

[17] John Dewey, *The Sources of a Science of Education* (New York: Horace Liveright, 1929), pp. 76–77.

49

precisely those that come to grips with the processes by which ideas become moving forces in the social world.

There is inevitably a gap between aspiration and achievement in education, and between ideal and reality. And there is frequently a gap between stated intentions and revealed preferences. Moreover, ideals are themselves commonly modified by circumstance. Nonetheless, they have a life and validity of their own and they influence education profoundly, however flawed their substance or imperfect their realization. They are well worth examining, debating, and improving, for there is much more to *paideia* than mere ideology.

V

THE ecological approach I have attempted to sketch here is neutral with respect to the aims of education. Family nurture is educative. Classroom instruction in mathematics is educative. Museum exhibits are educative. Factory apprenticeships are educative. The exchange of enthusiasms among adolescents is educative. Government propaganda is educative. And commercial advertising is educative. The point of the ecological model is to indicate the scope and complexity of the educational situation. Yet, there is no reason why values cannot be applied and judgments made. To what extent does an educational program or opportunity help individuals extend their horizons, heighten their sensibilities, and rationalize their actions? To what extent does it assist and encourage individuals to seek further education? Those familiar with Deweyan theory will recognize here the principle of growth: the end of education, Dewey asserted, is the growth of the individual human being, and there is nothing to which growth is relative save more growth and nothing to which education is subordinate save more education.[18]

The ecological approach also sheds additional light on the problems of progressive educators during the first three quarters of the present century. For, in actuality, two simultaneous developments dominated the American educational scene during that period: the first was the steady expansion and extension of schooling—in mission, scope, intensity, and clientele; the second was the revolution outside the schools—the revolution implicit in the rise of cinema, radio, and television and in the transformation of American family life to which they contributed. The two developments were in some respects contradictory. As my colleague Martin S. Dworkin has pointed out, they occasioned continuing tensions in the larger education of the public between the instruction of the media (in the form of popular entertainment) and the instruction of the schools—tensions with respect to style, substance, values, and aspirations. The progressives increasingly sensed the tensions—one need only consult the continuing debate between John Dewey and Walter Lippmann during the 1920s and 1930s over the sources and character of public opinion—but

[18] John Dewey, *Democracy and Education* (New York: Macmillan, 1916), p. 60. I discussed some of the philosophical difficulties associated with the growth metaphor in *The Genius of American Education* (Pittsburgh: University of Pittsburgh Press, 1965), pp. 30–36.

they were unable to conceptualize them adequately, much less resolve them. In the end, the progressives settled on the school as the crucial lever of social reform and individual self-realization at precisely the time when the basic configuration of American education had begun to shift radically. And the theoretical dilemma in which they found themselves may well have reflected their own awareness of the partial character of their solution. In any case, there was no way to resolve the dilemma apart from a fundamental theoretical reformulation.

That reformulation is now underway, primarily in Europe and largely under the aegis of UNESCO. It is manifest in a host of reports that have appeared since 1968 under various rubrics such as "lifelong education" or "recurrent education" or "l'éducation permanente." The reports recognize that education proceeds in many situations and through many institutions other than the school, that individuals are involved in education throughout the entire life span, that any realistic national or international planning for education must take account of these fundamental facts, and that for free societies the goals of such planning must be, first, to establish structures and methods that will assist individuals throughout their lives in maintaining the continuity of their apprenticeship and training and, second, to equip each individual "to become in the highest and truest degree both the object and the instrument of his own development through the many forms of self-education." True, in perusing this literature, one finds author after author tending to dwell on the traditional categories of schooling and "adult education." But there can be no denying the concerted effort to break out of historic molds. In ef-

Toward an Ecology of Education

fect, a body of theory is emerging that joins the kind of humane aspirations and social awareness that marked the progressive movement to a realistic understanding of the nature and character of present-day education. It is a promising time for the intellectual reformulation that must go hand in hand with social and institutional change.[19]

[19] Paul Lengrand, An Introduction to Lifelong Education (Paris: UNESCO, 1970), pp. 44–45. The literature on "lifelong education" or "recurrent education" or "l'éducation permanente" is substantial. There are useful bibliographies in the special number of the International Review of Education (20, no. 4 [1974]) devoted to "Lifelong Education and Learning Strategies" and in R. H. Dave, Lifelong Education and School Curriculum (Hamburg: UNESCO Institute for Education, 1973). Among better-conceived "models" are Seth Spaulding, "Life-long Education: A Modest Model for Planning and Research," Comparative Education 10 (1974): 101–13, and George W. Parkyn, Towards a Conceptual Model of Lifelong Education (Paris: UNESCO, 1973). Probably the best-known policy document to date is Edgar Faure et al., Learning to Be: The World of Education Today and Tomorrow (Paris: UNESCO, 1972), which, for all its breadth of vision, tends to focus almost exclusively on schools and classrooms. For the relation of lifelong education to national and international development, see the several essays in James R. Sheffield, ed., "New Perspectives on Education and International Development," Teachers College Record 76 (1974–75): 533–623. For an early American contribution, see Robert M. Hutchins, The Learning Society (New York: Praeger, 1968), with its interesting definition of education as "the organized, deliberate attempt to help people to become intelligent" (p. 51).

PUBLIC EDUCATION AND THE EDUCATION OF THE PUBLIC

WHAT WOULD BE the implications of an ecological view of education for the business of educational policy making? If the theory of education is indeed a theory of the relation of various educative interactions and institutions to one another and to the society at large, what is public education and how does public education relate to the public? Three ways of thinking about the problem suggest themselves, which might be referred to as thinking *comprehensively*, thinking *relationally*, and thinking *publicly* about education.

First, thinking comprehensively. We have traditionally assumed in the United States that the public school for more than a century created and recreated the American public virtually singlehandedly, and endowed that public with its unique ability to work cooperatively on social problems despite its ethnic, racial, religious, and social class heterogeneity. The assumption, of course, is not without foundation. The public school has labored mightily over the years to nurture certain common values and commitments and to teach the skills whereby a vastly variegated society can resolve its conflicts peacefully rather than by the methods of guerrilla warfare. Indeed, the public school has actually come to symbolize the quest for community in American society. But the public school has never functioned alone or in isolation. As I suggested earlier, where the public school has succeeded, it has functioned as part of a configuration of education that has usually included families, churches, and Sunday schools, all committed to similar or complementary values. Where the configuration has disintegrated, however, as it has from time to time in our larger cities, and when the centrifugal forces of heterogeneity have overbalanced the centripetal forces of community, the public school has been less successful. My assertion is not the powerlessness of public schooling—far from it—but rather its limitations. And the moral is simple: the public school ought never to take the entire credit for the educational accomplishments of the public, and it ought never to be assigned the entire blame.

The fact is that the public is educated by many institutions, some of them private and some of them public, and that public schools are only one among several important public institutions that educate the public. There are, after all, public libraries, public museums, public television, and public work projects (the most extensive of which are the military services). Other societies, of course, have used quite different agencies to educate the public. The Soviet Union, for example, has used the Komsomol, a network of youth organizations, as an important instrument of public education, while the People's Republic of China has used communes in public factories and on public farms in similar fashion. And the Indians, the Australians, and the Venezuelans have used public radio to teach literacy in areas remote from schools.

A kind of obverse of these propositions is the recognition that *all* educational transactions have both private and public consequences. Family nurture that encourages independence, church teaching that condemns family planning, industrial apprenticeships that exclude members of minority groups from participation, television news programs that dramatize the human consequences of military ventures—these are but examples of private educative efforts that have profound public impact.

In sum, then, to think comprehensively about education we must consider policies with respect to a wide variety of institutions that educate, not only schools and colleges, but libraries, museums, day-care centers, radio and television stations, offices, factories, and farms. To be concerned solely with schools, given the educational world we are living in today, is to have a kind of fortress mentality in contending with a very fluid and dynamic situation. Education must be looked at whole, across the entire life span, and in all the situations and institutions in which it occurs. Obviously, public policy will not touch and ought not to touch every situation with equal intensity—that happens only in totalitarian societies, and even in totalitarian societies it never happens quite as efficaciously as the leaders would prefer. Indeed there are some situations public policy will not touch at all. But it must at least consider each, so that wise choices can be made as to *where* to invest *what* effort to achieve *which* goals with respect to *which* clienteles. The United States Congress already does this when it decides to allocate so many dollars to children's television rather than schooling (and in dealing with children's television it inevitably affects the family). And local communities already do this when they decide in a period of budgetary stringency to close a public library rather than a public school. I would only insist that the range of possibilities be understood far more explicitly than it has been in the past and that public authorities approach these questions of allocation rationally rather than whimsically, with a full awareness of educational consequences.

Incidentally, the time-honored separation of school politics from general community politics in the United States has tended to hamper the kind of comprehensive analysis suggested here. The separation grew up for good and sufficient reason, namely, to insulate the schools from the worst of partisan controversy. Its unintended consequence in our own time, however, has too often been to frustrate attempts at collaboration among different educational institutions and authorities. John Henry Martin and Charles H. Harrison propose, in a recent book entitled *Free to Learn* (1972), the calling of "local educational conventions" as vehicles whereby citizens might inquire into the character and quality of the educational services available to themselves and their children. Such conventions would provide an arena for traditionally autonomous individuals and agencies (both public and private) to exchange ideas via a political instrument that would have no direct power beyond the power of discussion and recommendation—somewhat in the fashion of White House conferences in the areas of education and child welfare. Now, if the dialogue were genuine and if any recommendations that emerged truly flowed from the dialogue—which admittedly has not always been the case with White House conferences—then such conventions would be immensely helpful at all levels of the polity, as devices for stimulating interest in educational affairs at the same time as they conveyed information concerning the range and variety of educational programs. They would also doubtless serve the cause of comprehensive educational planning, though I think such planning should be undertaken by other agencies with more carefully defined responsibilities and more precisely designated powers.

II

BEYOND thinking comprehensively about education, we must think relationally. To do this means in the first instance to be aware of the problem of allocation of financial and human resources and of resultant educational outcomes. As indicated above, legislative bodies do this when they decide to spend a given amount of money on public television rather than public schooling, though too often such decisions result more from political pressure than from thoughtful deliberation concerning what educational outcomes are most desirable and what educational efforts are most likely to produce them.

Thinking relationally also means that, whenever an educational effort goes forward, it must do so not in isolation from other educative institutions but in relation to them. From the vantage point of the school, this is a significant principle. Given the thrust of my argument, I am occasionally accused of downgrading the school and being uninterested in schoolteachers. Nothing could be further from the truth. I am interested rather in making schools and schoolteachers more effective; and they will not be more effective until they become aware of and actually engage these other educators.

In some subject areas, of course, the school originates much of what it teaches. Mathematics is an example. In mathematics, the student learns much of what he needs to know for the first time in the classroom (though with the new mathematics series now being produced for television by the Education Development Center, that may become less and less true). But in other realms, languages and literature, for example, or social studies or hygiene, or the arts, or the domain of values and morals, the child has his first learning and possibly his most persuasive learning earlier and elsewhere. In these areas, it may be that the best the school can do is *engage* the instruction of the other educators and seek to strengthen or complement or correct or neutralize or countereducate or, most importantly, perhaps, try to develop in students an awareness of the other educators and an ability to deal with them on their own.

Actually, three recent reports on the education of American youth, sponsored, respectively, by the President's Science Advisory Committee (PSAC), the Kettering Foundation, and the

United States Office of Education, focus a good deal of attention on these questions of relation. What is striking about the reports, even in light of some overlap in the membership of the several commissions that prepared them, is the remarkable similarity of their diagnoses and recommendations. All three begin with an indictment of the present-day high school, picturing it as a severely troubled institution largely victimized by its own success. In less than a century, the reports argue, it has evolved from an elite institution designed to train a small proportion of adolescents along traditional academic lines into a popular institution enrolling ninety percent of American youth between the ages of fourteen and eighteen. In the process, however, it has managed increasingly to isolate young people from the rest of society, organizing them into rigidly defined age groups (freshmen, sophomores, juniors, seniors) that have little contact with either younger children or adults. In the language of one report, the schools have effectively "decoupled the generations." As a result, the reports conclude, the ordinary processes of socialization have been weakened, confused, and disjointed, and the symptoms are everywhere apparent—in the steady decline of academic standards in inner-city schools, in the growing irregularity of attendance at most schools, and in the rising incidence of theft, vandalism, personal assault, and general alienation in all schools.[1]

[1] *Youth: Transition to Adulthood: Report of the Panel on Youth of the President's Science Advisory Committee* (Chicago: University of Chicago Press, 1974); *The Reform of Secondary Education: A Report to the Public and the Profession by the National Commission on the Reform of Secondary Education, Established by the Charles F. Kettering Foundation* (New York: McGraw-Hill, 1973); and "The Education of Adolescents: Report of the National Panel on High Schools and Adolescent Education, United States Office of Education," mimeographed. The reference to "decoupling the generations" is from the Office of Education report, p. 6.

As a solution to these problems, the reports urge an opening up of the school system in the interest of recoupling the generations. The PSAC panel is probably the most far-reaching in its recommendations. It proposes that high schools be made smaller and more specialized, that students be permitted to attend more than one such specialized school, simultaneously or seriatim, and that the schools themselves experiment with ways of becoming agents for their students in arranging for appropriate education outside of school (in businesses, for example, or in child-care centers or in museums). The panel proposes, additionally, that a wide variety of work-study arrangements be developed, so that young people can continue part-time work or go back and forth between full-time study and full-time work. The panel further proposes that special government credit vouchers be devised, equivalent in value to the cost of a four-year college education, to be given to young people at the age of, say, sixteen, so that responsibility for their education from that time forward will be in their own hands. And the panel proposes, finally, that a wide range of residential and nonresidential youth facilities and public-service programs (such as the Peace Corps, VISTA, or the Neighborhood Youth Corps) be created, under government sponsorship and on an experimental basis, that would permit formal education and community service to proceed hand in hand.

As is often the case with public commission reports, there is a fundamental body of theory underlying many of the recommendations, in this instance the theory set forth in Urie Bronfenbrenner's 1970 study *Two Worlds of Childhood: U.S. and U.S.S.R.* Using comparative data on child rearing in Russia and the United States, Bronfenbrenner catalogued the many situations in which adults and children interact freely in Soviet families, neighborhood centers, schools, youth programs, farms, shops, factories, and government bureaus, with certain common civic and moral goals held constantly before them. He then pointed to the relative paucity of such interactions in the United States, where television watching and peer group activities have tended to replace adult-child associations. "As we read the evidence," Bronfenbrenner concluded, "both from our own research and that of others, we cannot escape the conclusion that, if the current trend persists, if the institutions of our society continue to remove parents, other adults, and older youth from active participation in the lives of children, and if the resulting vacuum is filled by the age-segregated peer group, we can anticipate increased alienation, indifference, antagonism, and violence on the part of the younger generation in all segments of our society—middle-class children as well as the disadvantaged." By way of remedying the disruptive trends in the process of socialization in American society, Bronfenbrenner recommended a series of reforms, all designed to increase opportunities for children to associate with adults in realistic social situations where they could undertake genuine responsibility for worthwhile tasks.[2]

Now, there is much in the reports and in the body of theory associated with them that is worthy of the most careful consid-

---

[2] Urie Bronfenbrenner, *Two Worlds of Childhood: U.S. and U.S.S.R.* (New York: Russell Sage Foundation, 1970), pp. 116–17 (italics removed). See also James S. Coleman's influential monograph *The Adolescent Society* (Glencoe, Ill.: The Free Press, 1961).

eration. I for one would object to some of their apocalyptic rhetoric—the references to schools as "beleaguered institutions" or "aging vats," the expression of unqualified (and often uncritical) faith in alternative opportunities of every sort and variety. I would be concerned also with a certain hypostasizing of "youth," a tendency to refer to youth as a clearly defined stage with certain clearly defined problems and needs that are apparently quite different from those of "childhood" and "early adulthood" (a paradoxical theoretical counterpart, perhaps, to the very isolation of youth so roundly deplored). And most seriously, I would criticize the use of socialization as a single lens through which to assess the entire program of schooling. The PSAC report charges that most high schools are "incomplete contexts" for maturation. One might respond that the statement is a truism, for presumably young people also mature in interaction with families, churches, peers, libraries, and a host of other educative institutions, as indeed they ought to. Moreover, socialization is only one aim of the educative process, and a partial and problematical one at that. It too must be judged against the criterion of individual growth, and, while there can be no fruitful conception of individual growth apart from a well-defined conception of social context, socialization is an instrumental rather than an ultimate goal.[3]

---

[3] The reference to the high school as "a beleaguered institution" is from the Kettering report, p. 8; the phrase "aging vats" is from the Office of Education report, p. 6. The discussion alluded to in the PSAC report is on p. 2. One can also raise problems with Bronfenbrenner's comparative analysis of Soviet and American patterns of socialization in the extent to which he downplayed—though he did not ignore—those differences that derive from the more stringent and far-reaching modes of politi-

These criticisms notwithstanding, the several reports do direct attention to the relationships between schooling and familial education, television education, and vocational education. They do ask the school to serve as broker between its own programs and the educational programs of other agencies, thereby mitigating the danger of exploitation inherent in blanket schemes to reduce the period of compulsory schooling. And they do put forward a fruitful conception of self-education, reinforcing it with the proposal for a government educational voucher. In these respects, the reports go far beyond most in exemplifying relational thinking.

Everything that has been said about relationalism with respect to the schools also holds, of course, for the other educators. For day-care workers, pastors, editors of children's encyclopedias, and directors of senior citizens' centers, the message is the same: whatever is done, to be effective, must be done with an awareness of what has gone on and what is going on elsewhere. Actually, since many of these educators operate in the open market and are supported by clients' fees, they

---

cal control in the Soviet Union. There is simply more freedom to differ publicly in matters of opinion and behavior in the United States, in part because a more restricted range of social and intellectual affairs is defined as "political," and that in and of itself creates a more dissonant context for socialization. The point is significant; for, if a utopian society is one whose values and institutions are perfectly consonant and complementary, so also—at least in the ideal of the ruler(s)—is a totalitarian society. Liberty in its very nature is disruptive of that consonance and complementarity, and hence disruptive of the processes of socialization. But its promise, of course, is freedom, or genuine choice among alternatives. Put another way, what disrupts can also simultaneously enrich. The problem for a democratic society is one of achieving and maintaining an appropriate balance among the several values involved; and my point here is that continuing public discussion of what is an appropriate balance and how to maintain it is crucial.

have been somewhat more assiduous than school people about understanding and strengthening their relations with other institutions, if for no other reason, on grounds of prudence. Thus, day-care centers work closely with families, children's publishers consult diligently with the schools; senior citizens' centers stay in touch with local recreation facilities; and churches and synagogues make it their business to collaborate with all of these institutions.

Finally, it should be noted that relational thinking has special relevance for educational evaluation and accountability, since any judgment of a particular educational program must be made in light of what is going on elsewhere that affects that program. This is the real message of the Coleman and Jencks studies of equal educational opportunity, not that the school is power*less* but that the family is power*ful*. Given the prominence of schooling in our present-day conception of education, the school tends to get all the blame or all the praise for educational outcomes. Frequently, when a youngster enters school with a deficit, whether in knowledge or, more importantly, in the techniques and habits of learning, the school may make a Herculean effort that will result in very modest gains on the achievement scales, but the school gets blamed for a bad performance. Conversely, a youngster may enter school with a great deal of knowledge and a well-nurtured ability to seek out knowledge, both of which have been learned at home and from peers of similar background, and the school may make a modest effort which shows up brilliantly on the achievement scales, but the school gets all the credit. One of my colleagues likes to tell a story about a school for tall men, for which the admission requirement is to be six feet in height. The school graduates a large number of tall men and assumes full responsibility for its remarkable achievement.

III

FINALLY, we must think publicly about education. This implies several things. To begin, it means we must be aware that public thinking about education and public policy making for education go on at a variety of levels and in a variety of places. They go forward at the local, state, regional, federal, and international levels, and they proceed in legislatures, in the courts, in executive agencies, and in private and quasi-public civic organizations. The political struggle over busing as a device for achieving racial integration in the schools is an excellent example, as is the battle to persuade the Federal Communications Commission to adopt more stringent rules for the governance of children's television.

The growing reliance on the courts during the past quarter-century to develop policies through the definition, assertion, and claim of certain social and educational rights is also profoundly relevant. It is an oft-repeated truism that the courts have been our most influential agencies of educational policy making since World War II. But, as John Coons has pointed out, courts tend to stress our differences: they tend to affirm the rights of individuals or groups to dissent from agreed upon policies. Legislatures, on the other hand, tend to deal with the definition and advancement of that which is common. Hence, the growing recourse to the courts in matters of educational policy is fraught with significance, substantively as well as procedurally. And it is fraught with significance for the polity itself. As my former teacher Henry Steele Commager, certainly second to none in his insistent espousal of the cause of civil liberties, pointed out some years ago in a discussion of *Majority Rule and Minority Rights*, recourse to the courts, particularly in the realm of constitutional law, is an immensely powerful tool in a democratic society for the achievement of short-term goals, especially with respect to the redress of civil and political inequity. But recourse to the courts short-circuits certain educational processes vital to the long-range development of a democratic society. There is, after all, little opportunity for appeal once the court of last resort has handed down its ruling, and the public receives precious little political education in the course of appellate proceedings. This is not to say that the Warren court and the Burger court have not tried at many points to educate the public with respect to the bearing of the Constitution on education. It is only to argue, with Commager, that the legislative process, along with the public debate surrounding it, is a surer and more fundamental long-range educator of the public than the judicial process.[4]

I should add quite explicitly at this point that nothing here should be taken as a criticism of the political outcomes of recourse to the federal and state courts, from Brown in 1954, to Serrano in 1971 and Robinson in 1973, to Goss in 1975. It is merely to argue that the process of public education result-

---

[4] Henry Steele Commager, *Majority Rule and Minority Rights* (New York: Oxford University Press, 1943), chap. 2.

ing from court decisions is very different from the process that leads to the enactment and implementation of legislation. And the current turmoil over school busing in Boston, the failure of the legislatures in California and New Jersey to accomplish the mandated reforms of their respective state systems of school finance, and the puzzlement that has followed the more recent Goss ruling on the rights of pupils, are illustrative of this fact.[5]

The distinction between the politics of the courts and the politics of legislatures brings me to my last point, namely, that given the range and variety of institutions that educate the public, some of them public, some of them quasi-public, and some of them private, simplistic notions of public control become untenable. Control, after all, varies in character and intensity from the kind of direct supervision one sees in the management of public school systems or public libraries, to the kind of regulation exercised over the television industry by the Federal Communications Commission, to the kind of influence tax policy exerts on the size and structure of families and hence on the nature of familial education. And, if one looks at the power of the educative agencies farthest removed from the public reach, one is led, not to deny the need for effective public regulation of public schools, public libraries, and public television, but to affirm the need for public discussion in the areas beyond the sphere of direct public control. Hence, we are thrown, inevitably, back to the politics of per-

[5] Brown v. Board of Education, 347 U.S. 483 (1954); Serrano v. Priest, Cal., 487 P2d 1241 (1971); Robinson v. Cahill, 62 N.J. 473 (1973); Goss v. Lopez, U.S., 42 L Ed 2d 725 (1975).

suasion and to the public dialogue about educational means and ends that is the essence of the politics of persuasion.[6]

We live in an age that affirms individuality and pluralism, and, given what governments, including democratic governments, have done with their power in our time, one can understand and sympathize with the attractiveness of such affirmation. Yet, if Dewey taught us anything, it was that the public good is something more than the sum total of private goods and that a viable community is more than a collection of groups, each occupying its own turf and each doing its own thing. Indeed, *Democracy and Education* is as much a work of social theory as it is of educational theory, and Dewey's own position is strikingly clear: there must be ample room in a democratic society for a healthy individualism and a healthy pluralism, but that individualism and that pluralism must also partake of a continuing quest for community. In fact, individuality itself is only liberated and fully realized as the individual interacts with an ever widening variety of communities. Recall Dewey's classic paragraph:

A democracy is more than a form of government; it is primarily a mode of associated living, of conjoint communicated experience. The extension in space of the number of individuals who participate in an interest so that each has to refer his own action to that of

---

[6] On the politics of persuasion and the role of "publics" or interest groups in the politics of persuasion, see John Dewey, *The Public and Its Problems: An Essay in Political Inquiry* (New York: Henry Holt, 1927) and *Liberalism and Social Action* (New York: G. P. Putnam's Sons, 1935); David B. Truman, *The Governmental Process: Political Interests and Public Opinion*, 2d ed. (New York: Alfred A. Knopf, 1971); and Stephen K. Bailey, *Education Interest Groups in the Nation's Capital* (Washington, D.C.: American Council on Education, 1975). The Bailey book limits its attention to the development of policy regarding schools and colleges.

others, and to consider the action of others to give point and direction to his own, is equivalent to the breaking down of those barriers
of class, race, and national territory which kept men from perceiving
the full import of their activity. These more numerous and more
varied points of contact denote a greater diversity of stimuli to which
an individual has to respond; they consequently put a premium on
variation in his action. They secure a liberation of powers which
remain suppressed as long as the incitations to action are partial, as
they must be in a group which in its exclusiveness shuts out many
interests.[7]

Now, there are some who have always suspected Dewey of
having done away with individuality entirely in this social
formulation of the self. Horace Kallen and T. V. Smith in
particular, both liberals of Dewey's own philosophical persuasion, felt obliged to dissociate themselves from Dewey's
conception and to explicate the realm of the private, the soli-
tary, and the unshared, which they saw as the essence of self-
hood. Dewey remained appreciative but unmoved, continuing to believe that individuals would always be the "center and
consummation of experience" but that "what the individual
actually *is* in his life experience depends upon the nature and

[7] John Dewey, *Democracy and Education* (New York: Macmillan, 1916), p. 101.
The classic American work on pluralism is Horace M. Kallen, *Culture and Democracy in the United States* (New York: Boni and Liveright, 1924). On the new plural-
ism, see William Greenbaum, "America in Search of a New Ideal: An Essay on the
Rise of Pluralism," *Harvard Educational Review* 64 (1974): 411–40, and Charles A.
Tesconi, Jr., *Schooling in America: A Social Philosophical Analysis* (Boston:
Houghton Mifflin, 1975), chaps. 11–13. On pluralism and the problems of the public,
see Thomas F. Green, *Education and Pluralism: Ideal and Reality* (Syracuse: School
of Education, Syracuse University, 1966) and "Citizenship or Certification," in
Murray L. Wax, Stanley Diamond, and Fred O. Gearing, *Anthropological Perspec-
tives on Education* (New York: Basic Books, 1971). On the problem of nurturing community, see Joseph J. Schwab, "Learning Community," *The Center Magazine* 8
(May–June 1975): 30–44.

PUBLIC EDUCATION

movement of associated life." I myself find nothing in Dewey's
idea of individuality that would preclude the self-conscious
reflectiveness one associates with personal autonomy. Dewey
merely insisted that whatever individuality is will depend ultimately upon the social context in which individuality comes
to be, and indeed his insistence serves as a useful antidote to
various forms of romanticism and mysticism that would reify
the self and isolate it from the multifarious relationships that
give it meaning. [8]

How, then, do we achieve an appropriate balance between
the demands of individuality and the demands of community?
I have a very simple starting point, to which I think there is no
alternative. We converse—informally in small groups and
more formally through organizations via systematic political
processes. The proper education of the public and indeed the
proper creation of "publics" will not go forward in our society
until we undertake anew a great public dialogue about education. In fact, I would maintain that the questions we need to
ask about education are among the most important questions
that can be raised in our society, particularly at this juncture in
its history. What knowledge should "we the people" hold in
common? What values? What skills? What sensibilities?
When we ask such questions, we are getting to the heart of the
kind of society we want to live in and the kind of society we

[8] Horace Kallen, *Individualism: An American Way of Life* (New York: Liveright,
1933) and "Individuality, Individualism, and John Dewey," *The Antioch Review* 19
(1959): 299–314; T. V. Smith, "The Double Discipline of Democracy," *The Virginia
Quarterly Review* 27 (1951): 515–27; John Dewey's credo in Clifton Fadiman, ed., *I
Believe: The Personal Philosophies of Certain Eminent Men and Women of Our Time*
(New York: Simon and Schuster, 1939), p. 347.

want our children to live in. We are getting to the heart of the kind of public we would like to bring into being and the qualities we would like that public to display. We are getting to the heart of the kind of community we need for our many individualities to flourish.[9]

Two thousand years ago, Aristotle wrote that when we educate we aim at the good life, and, since men and women disagree in their notions of the good life, they will disagree in their notions of education. The assertion is as true today as it was two thousand years ago. Obviously, men and women of goodwill are going to disagree about education. What is important about public education is that we work through to certain agreements about values and policies. We do not simply Balkanize the world; we also decide on common ground. We do that in the public schools, in public libraries, and over certain programs on public television because we have a notion of the kind of society we want our children to grow up in and live in. It's not that we're going to do away with different life-styles and different beliefs, or with the educational institutions—both public and private—that keep those different life-styles and beliefs alive. It's that we must practice those different life-styles and beliefs within a common framework of mutual respect and understanding. So often in recent years we have cast the choice as one between a full-blown and segregationist ethnicity on the one hand and some plastic, lowest-common-denominator community on the other. I would re-

---

[9] On the matter of conversing, one is reminded of a remark John Dewey made on his ninetieth birthday: "Democracy begins in conversation." See Corliss Lamont, ed., *Dialogue on John Dewey* (New York: Horizon Press, 1959), p. 88.

ject both in favor of new modes of thought that would permit—nay, encourage—maximum variation within certain agreed upon policies. I think we have the models in the alternative programs that have grown up in our contemporary public schools, public libraries, and public television systems, and I think we should develop, share, and publicize those models. In the last analysis, the most important dimension of the politics of education is the business of debating and defining the various forms those models might take and the various curricula they might teach. Moreover, the debate over what knowledge, what values, what skills, and what sensibilities we might want to nurture in the young and how we might want to nurture them is more important than the particular decisions we happen to reach at any given time. For the debate educates, and that education will affect the entire apparatus by which the public itself is created and renewed.

My conclusions, of course, are vintage Dewey. Recall that in the pedagogical creed he wrote for *The School Journal* in 1897, he argued that "education is the fundamental method of social progress and reform" and that "all reforms which rest simply upon the enactment of law, or the threatening of certain penalties, or upon changes in mechanical or outward arrangements, are transitory and futile." In the last analysis, the fundamental mode of politics in a democratic society is education, and it is in *that* way over all others that the educator is ultimately projected into politics. What is apparent here is the ancient prophetic role which Dewey himself had in mind when he wrote in 1897 that the teacher is always "the prophet of the true God" and "the usherer in of the true kingdom of

God." The millennialist tone of these phrases has always left me a bit uncomfortable, but the insight is nonetheless profound. Prophesy: in its root meaning, the calling of a people, via criticism and affirmation, to their noblest traditions and aspirations. Prophesy, I would submit, is the essential public function of the educator in a democratic society.[10]

[10] John Dewey, "My Pedagogic Creed," in Martin S. Dworkin, ed., *Dewey on Education* (New York: Teachers College Press, 1959), pp. 30, 32.

SCHOOLS OF

THE PROPHETS

PROPHESYING, as the early Puritan settlers of New England were wont to point out, is an arduous undertaking, not for the timid, the untutored, or the enthusiastic. It requires commitment, concern, and well-formed habits of study and reflection. Yet the Puritans considered prophesying—by which they meant public teaching—so important to the commonwealth that they founded Harvard College as a "school of the prophets" less than ten years after the initial settlement of the Massachusetts Bay Colony, assigning it substantial revenues at a time when Massachusetts was barely managing to maintain a subsistence economy. As Samuel Eliot Morison once remarked, there has been no comparable achievement in the history of modern colonization.

Now, it was Harvard College in its entirety that assumed the responsibility for the training of public teachers, not some part of Harvard; and so it was with William and Mary, Yale, Princeton, and the other fledgling colleges of early America. For one thing, all of them were relatively small, even by contemporary standards, so that extensive division of labor was simply not possible; but, even more importantly, the fragmentation of colleges and universities that was later to accompany the emergence of the modern fields of knowledge had not yet occurred, and, except for medicine, law, and divinity, there was little in the way of specialized professional instruction. It is only during the last hundred years that schools and departments of education as we know them today have come into being, largely as training schools for the teachers and leaders of the burgeoning public school system. And as is well known, these schools and departments have been dominated by the concerns of their clients. In fact, they have been essentially schools and departments of schooling. Their teaching and research have been devoted almost exclusively to preparing personnel for the schools and extending knowledge about the schools. Their theories and methods have been based almost entirely on data drawn from the schools, and indeed these theories and methods have derived primarily from experiments that conceive of the schools as isolated institutions educating children who are not influenced by parents, pastors, peers, or the marketplace.

The question then arises, How might the ecological approach that has been propounded here bear on the education of educators? Or, What might "schools of the prophets" look like during the last quarter of the twentieth century? Two alternatives come to mind: a broadened school of education, or a university broadly focused on education. With respect to the former, several suggestions occur. In the first place, to repeat themes sounded earlier, a modern school of education ought to look at education comprehensively, and this means considering the educative process across the entire life span, in all the situations and institutions in which it occurs, in a wide variety of social and cultural contexts, and in the past as well as in the present and alternatively imagined futures. In the second place, a modern school of education ought to look at education relationally, and this means viewing each educational transaction or situation in relation to all the other educational transactions or situations that inevitably affect it. Educators learned during the 1930s and 1940s to accept as a truism that education must always be seen in its broader social and political context (the theory of education is a theory of school and society). Now, in addition to that—though not in place of it—they must also consider any particular effort at education in its broader educational context (the theory of education is a theory of the relation of various educative interactions and institutions to one another and to society at large).

On the side of training, this implies a radical redefinition and relocation of effort. It means that the school of education must become directly concerned with all the roles, occupations, and professions that are involved with education. It must professionalize or further professionalize some of these—day-care workers, for example—and it must certainly illuminate all of them. Moreover, the illumination must be both in the realm of science (I have in mind such propositions as, "If you do A there is an eighty percent chance you are going to get outcome B") and in the realm of values (I allude to such questions as, "Is outcome B desirable in the first place, and if so why?"). In other words, there should be intellectual light and substance in the school of education, not only for schoolteachers and college professors, but also for parents, librarians, curators, and publishers.

With respect to curriculum, it means that courses of study should draw their problems, their data, and their examples from a variety of educational situations and that practice teaching and field instruction should be undertaken in a broad range of educational institutions. Moreover, since educational relations extend in time and in space, it also means that persons preparing to teach should be afforded experience with more than one type of educational institution, with more than one kind of clientele, and with more than one particular age group—the rotating internship of medical training is a useful paradigm.

Obviously, in all of this the faculty of education will have to work closely not only with the faculty of letters and science (such collaboration has often been urged in our time) but also with the faculties of social work, journalism, and divinity. Those faculties have long been in the business of preparing educators, and nothing in my argument for comprehensiveness should be taken to imply some new effort on the part of the school or department of education to reach out for every single task in the university. On the other hand, those faculties have not always been as sophisticated as they might be in the educational theories and principles they have propounded. I think social workers might profit from viewing the family as an educational institution rather than merely as a unit requiring treatment; I think clergymen might render their moral teaching more effective if they took more seriously the implications of modern learning theory; and I suspect journalists might learn a good deal about the problems of popularizing without vulgarizing if they studied the curriculum reform movement of the last twenty years. In short, my case is for collaboration, not preemption. The point is to think relationally, not imperialistically.

On the side of scholarship, conceiving of education comprehensively and relationally implies the mounting of an educational research and development program that at its best would dwarf the effort of the 1960s. The fact is that popular education is a comparatively recent phenomenon in human history and that for all our supposedly massive efforts at research and development over the past decade we know comparatively little about it. For most of human history, men and women have believed that only an elite is worthy and capable of education and that the great mass of people should be trained as hewers of wood and drawers of water, if they are to be trained at all. It was only at the end of eighteenth century and beginning of the nineteenth that popular leaders in Europe and America—the Marquis de Condorcet in France, Thomas Jefferson in the United States, and Lord Brougham in England—began to dream of universal school systems that would give everyone a chance to partake of the arts and sciences. Not surprisingly, they had their most immediate successes with the children who were easiest to teach—those who through early nurture in the family and other institutions had been prepared for whatever it was that the school had to offer.

Now, in the twentieth century, we have turned to the more difficult task, the education of those at the margins—those who suffer from physical, mental, or emotional handicaps, those who have long been held at a distance by political or social means, and those who for a variety of other reasons are less ready for what the school has to offer and hence more difficult to teach. At the same time, we are beginning to relearn the truism that schools are not the only institutions where teaching goes on. We know with respect to the very young, for example, that, unless some things are done within the family during the first years of life, all teaching in the later years will be more difficult. We know with respect to adolescents that hard-core illiterates with whom the schools have failed miserably can become literate in a matter of months, in camplike situations where materials have been specially prepared, learning opportunities have been properly arranged, and the personal benefits of literacy and other skills have been fully comprehended. We know with respect to the middle-aged that it is easier to teach many things at the place of work than it is to teach them in a classroom somewhere else—this insight was at the heart, incidentally, of one of the most imaginative innovations in the history of American education, the agricultural extension service. And we know with respect to older people that continued learning can literally come to mean the difference between life and death, that some things, like poetry and drama, that made no sense in high school and college suddenly make a great deal of sense and that it is easier to pursue those things in informal clubs rather than in formal classrooms, in the company of others rather than at home alone.

The fact is that to be intelligent about education in the years ahead we are going to have to build a body of theory that draws its data and its concepts from all the institutions that educate, that leads us to methods and techniques appropriate to each, and that helps us design programs for the particular agencies and the particular stages of life where they will be most efficient and most effective. And the research programs of our schools and departments of education across the country are going to be crucial in the development of such a body of theory. We need to reconcile and synthesize immense masses of data that are currently classified as "socialization" in one part of the university, "enculturation" in another part of the university, and "learning" in still another part of the university. Hence, the necessity once again for the closest possible intellectual relations between the faculty of education and certain other academic and professional departments. We need to find out why one family nurtures curiosity more effectively than another, why two siblings in the same family manifest very different levels and styles of curiosity, and why a youngster who is curious about everything at home sometimes manifests massive indifference to everything at school. We need to find out why some churches and some libraries are crowded with interested adults every evening in the week while others remain empty. We need to determine the balance between edification and entertainment that marks a successful children's educational program on television and then determine the quite different balance between edification and entertainment that marks a successful adult educational program. We need to study the teaching styles of an Alistair Cooke, or a Kenneth Clark, or a Jacob Bronowski, or a John Chancellor and see what we can learn from them, not only for teaching via television, but also for teaching in colleges, museums, and adult education centers. And, similarly, we need to review the experience of the successful Job Corps training centers during the late 1960s and see what we can learn from them for use in reformatories, prisons, and halfway houses.

Once we begin to find answers to these questions, we need to learn much more than we now know about how to get people to make use of the answers. There are still parents who prod their children relentlessly, thinking that prodding will nurture curiosity. There are still television programs that bore viewers mercilessly, thinking that viewers will learn something despite the boredom. There are still librarians who lock their books away on closed shelves, thinking that people will ask for the keys. And there are still prison systems that keep inmates idle and isolated, thinking that idleness will lead them to productive lives.

Also, we need to develop much better techniques than we now have for monitoring and assessing what we have accomplished in education. For all our sophistication in testing—and we have made tremendous strides in the last decade or so—our instruments are still imprecise about what should be evaluated and to what purpose. They deal almost exclusively with the cognitive aspects of learning. They tend to separate individuals for purposes of selection rather than providing information on the performance of the education system as a whole. And they tell us next to nothing about where anything in particular has been learned, about the relation between what is learned in one institution and what is learned in another, about how different individuals synthesize what they have learned in various institutions, and about what might be the best possible combinations of institutions for teaching particular kinds of knowledge or skills. Surely we are capable of better, given the sophisticated techniques our psychologists, sociologists, anthropologists, and educators have worked out over the past half-century for understanding and appraising human behavior.

Finally, a word about values, which are, after all, of the essence in prophesying. My late mentor, George S. Counts, stated the problem tersely in his magnum opus, *Education and American Civilization* (1952). "There is no quick and easy road to a great education," he wrote. "There is no simple device or formula for the achievement of this goal. Such an education cannot be derived from a study of the process itself, nor can it be found in the interests of children or in any number of 'great books.' It can come only from a bold and creative confronting of the nature, the values, the conditions, and the potentialities of a civilization. An education can rise no higher than the conception of the civilization that pervades it, gives it substance, and determines its purposes and direction." Along with studies of the modes and processes of education, a modern school of education must cultivate informed and imaginative visions of what education might mean in a truly humane society—a democratic society, committed to the dignity of all human beings and the worth of their individual lives; a free society, wherein each and every person is afforded a rich and varied opportunity to develop his or her potential to the fullest; a transnational society, which conceives its public life as extending to every man, woman, and child on what Barbara Ward and Buckminster Fuller have referred to as "spaceship earth." [1]

There has been a good deal of shrill rhetoric about such visions in recent years, but rather less reflection and dialogue. The commitment to equality has been loudly and ubiquitously affirmed, for example, but too often in isolation from its companion values of liberty and fraternity, with the result that the public has come slowly to believe the grotesque assertion that the schools have somehow failed because they have not made Americans equal. In similar fashion, the value of ecstasy has been widely celebrated as a primary goal of education, but too often in isolation from such companion values as resoluteness, responsibility, and forbearance, with the result once again that the public has come to accept assertions of educational failure because the schools have produced insufficient ecstasy. Too often, the prophet has been the enthusiast, proffering millennial hopes and grim forebodings rather than reasoned expectations derived from systematic reflection on past and present experience. [2]

The kinds of training, research, and reflection proposed

---

[1] George S. Counts, *Education and American Civilization* (New York: Bureau of Publications, Teachers College, Columbia University, 1952), p. 36.

[2] Christopher Jencks *et al.*, *Inequality: A Reassessment of the Effect of Family and Schooling in America* (New York: Basic Books, 1972); George B. Leonard, *Education and Ecstasy* (New York: Delacorte Press, 1968).

here should prove key elements in enabling schools of education to create a new kind of educational leadership for the country at the local, state, regional, and national levels— leaders able to consider educational policy whole, leaders able to wrestle with the crucial questions surrounding the allocation of educational resources and educational tasks among different educational institutions, leaders able to assist the public in mounting the kind of discussion of educational aims and policies that is essential to a democratic society. The level of public discussion of educational affairs in recent years has left much to be desired: it has too often been trivial and uninformed or, worse yet, as I have suggested, misinformed by shoddy scholarship. But the fault is not with the public, it is rather with the educational professions, which have failed to define the issues more profoundly, more realistically, and more engagingly. I think a more fruitful definition of issues needs to be undertaken, and I think one of its major sources will lie in revitalized schools and departments of education across the country.

II

A BROADENED SCHOOL of education, then, which views education comprehensively and relationally, provides one model of a modern school of the prophets. The other model is the university itself, with its attention broadly focused on education. Now, there is something almost ludicrous about arguing that universities should focus on education, and yet the fact is that they have not done so in the modern era. Quite the contrary: they have tended to avoid comprehensive questions of education as too disruptive internally, preferring to leave them to schools and departments of education (which have dealt with them partially at best) or to outside agencies. Yet the very scope and character of the research and training programs I have described makes them inevitably matters of university-wide concern. The several behavioral science departments (particularly anthropology, biology, psychology, and sociology) will clearly have a stake in any systematic research into the processes of education. The professional schools of human services (from medicine to social work) will surely be interested in the contribution of education to public health and welfare, while the professional schools of management (from business to public administration) will be similarly interested in the political economy of the education system. And the various departments of arts and sciences will obviously have a double concern, with their own perpetuation and advancement through effective graduate training, on the one hand, and with the popularization of their distinctive subject matter, on the other. As Matthew Arnold observed more than a century ago, no field of culture (or scholarship) in the modern world can ignore its responsibility to humanize its findings, to synthesize and order them in a fashion that renders them publicly teachable and comprehensible.

The university's concern, however, goes beyond this. Dewey observed in *Democracy and Education* that the worth of any social institution should be measured by its effect in "enlarging and improving experience" or, alternatively, that "the ultimate value of every institution is its distinctively human effect—its effect upon conscious experience." He was stating there an instrumental view of institutions, namely, that in the ideal democratic society institutions come to be judged by the extent to which they are truly educative. Now, one criticism of the definition of education I have propounded here is that its stress on intentionality too easily blinds us to the educative effects of the law, literature, and the arts. I would reply to the contrary. The law, literature, and the arts inevitably shape human beings, willy-nilly, for good or ill. But it is only when lawmakers, authors, and artists become deliberate and self-conscious about their efforts, with conceptions in mind of desirable outcomes in human beings, that they become true educators. And, obversely, it is only when citizens come self-consciously to the law, literature, and the arts, with the aim of their own self-development in view, that their efforts become truly educative. In the absence of such intentionality and self-consciousness about goals and processes, on one side or the other but ideally on both, there is no education, merely influence. And, while the influence of the law, literature, and the arts is doubtless profound, that influence is not necessarily educative.[3]

Once such assertions are granted, the university's involvement in public education becomes total and inescapable. Its alumni will be judged not only according to their capacity for continued self-education; they will be judged, even more importantly, according to their capacity to participate in and lead

[3] John Dewey, *Democracy and Education* (New York: Macmillan, 1916), pp. 7, 8.

institutions that are essentially educative. Thus, lawyers are potentially educators, artists are potentially educators—all institutional leaders are potentially educators. Whether or not they fulfill that potential depends in large measure on the knowledge and skills and, most significantly, on the values and commitments they have learned at the university. If the university has taught them only knowledge and skills, whether or not that knowledge and those skills are dignified with the high-sounding label "professional," it will not have made them educators. Nor, for that matter, will it have educated them properly for service in a democratic society.

III

CLARK KERR, in his 1963 Godkin Lectures, subsequently published as *The Uses of the University*, traced the successive transformations of the modern university from the academic cloister idealized by John Henry Newman, to the research organism portrayed by Abraham Flexner, to the loosely bound multiversity typified by the University of California during Kerr's own administration there, and then went on to raise the ultimate question as to whether intellect could be the salvation of modern society. His answer was equivocal. He lamented the co-optation of the multiversity by national governments around the world but viewed the process as irresistible and irreversible; he could only hope that the multiversity would in turn humanize politics and serve as a bridge between East and West. Meanwhile, he saw no alternative to the relentless forward movement of organized scholarship, and concluded his discussion with a prescient observation from Alfred North Whitehead's *The Aims of Education* (1929):

In the conditions of modern life, the rule is absolute, the race which does not value trained intelligence is doomed. Not all your heroism, not all your social charm, not all your wit, not all your victories on land or at sea, can move back the finger of fate. To-day we maintain ourselves. To-morrow science will have moved forward yet one more step, and there will be no appeal from the judgment which will then be pronounced on the uneducated.[4]

The disenchantment of the 1970s with education in general and with universities in particular seems eons away from even the guarded optimism of Kerr's analysis. We have gone to the moon. We have harnessed the atom to peaceful purposes. We have developed simple and inexpensive forms of contraception, freeing women from the burden of unwanted pregnancy. We have all but eradicated poliomyelitis from the United States. And we have made substantial inroads against world hunger through the so-called green revolution. And the multiversity has been in the vanguard of every single one of these advances. Yet the disenchantment is pervasive. One can trace it to many sources—the failure of the economy to keep pace with the possibilities of scientific and technological progress, the disillusionment attending the war in Southeast Asia, the unrealistic expectations of students and taxpayers concerning the costs and benefits of college training, and, most important perhaps, a widespread sense of drift and purposelessness in ed-

---

[4] Alfred North Whitehead, *The Aims of Education and Other Essays,* reprint ed. (New York: The Free Press, 1967), p. 14.

ucation, in the face of which continued development would appear problematical at best.[5]

There is no reason to believe, however, that public confidence cannot be restored, given a worthwhile debate over ends and means and the renewed sense of commitment one might expect to emerge from it. And it is such a debate that I would call upon educators themselves to stimulate and define. To this end, it is instructive to read on in *The Aims of Education* to the passages just beyond the one quoted by Kerr, for they actually hold the key to resolving Kerr's equivocation. "We can be content," Whitehead cautions, "with no less than the old summary of educational ideal which has been current at any time from the dawn of our civilization. The essence of education is that it be religious." And Whitehead then explicates:

> A religious education is an education which inculcates duty and reverence. Duty arises from our potential control over the course of events. Where attainable knowledge could have changed the issue, ignorance has the guilt of vice. And the foundation of reverence is this perception, that the present holds within itself the complete sum of existence, backwards and forwards, that whole amplitude of time, which is eternity.

The convergence with Dewey, here as elsewhere, is striking: the function of the educator, once again, is prophesy, or the artistic linking of tradition and aspiration.[6]

The fact is that intellect as embodied in the university can-

[5] Nathan Glazer, "Who Wants Higher Education, Even When It's Free?" *The Public Interest*, no. 39 (Spring 1975): 130–35.

[6] Whitehead, *Aims of Education*, p. 14.

not save modern society in any redemptive sense, but it can and should serve society in helping to define and realize legitimate social aspirations. And social aspirations become legitimate in the extent to which they derive from broad public deliberation that is reflective on social experience and on the bearing of that experience on individual growth. "The present is all there is," Whitehead once observed. "It is holy ground; for it is the past, and it is the future." It is the ground that the educator must occupy in calling the public to the definition of *paideia*.[7]

[7] Whitehead, *Aims of Education*, p. 3.

INDEX

Adams, Henry, 42
Adler, Richard, 23n
aims of education, 50–53, 91, 95–96
Allport, Gordon W., 38
American Tract Society, 31
anarchism and education, 20n
Aristotle, 75
Arnold, Matthew, 92
assessment of education, 62, 68–69, 88–89

Bailey, Stephen K., 72n
Bailyn, Bernard, 28
benevolent society (as educator), 29
Berkhofer, Robert F., 28
Bettelheim, Bruno, 45–46
Bonhoeffer, Dietrich, 16
Boulding, Kenneth E., 45n
Boydston, Jo Ann, 8n
Bremer, John, 10
Bronfenbrenner, Urie, 64
Bronowski, Jacob, 88
Brougham, Henry Peter, 85
Brown v. Board of Education, 70–71
Bruner, Jerome S., 32

Carnegie Corporation of New York, xi, 11, 12, 15
Cater, Douglass, 23n
Center for International Documentation (Cuernavaca, Mexico), 15–16
Chancellor, John, 88
church (as educator), viii, 22, 29, 31, 33–35, 36, 67, 68, 87
cinema (as educator), 51
Clark, Kenneth, 88
Coleman, James S., 47, 68
Commager, Henry Steele, 70
commonsense analysis, 44–45

community, vii–viii, 33–36, 72–77
community center (as educator), 65, 67, 68
Condorcet, Marie Jean Antoine Nicholas de Caritat, Marquis de, 85
configuration of education, vii, 30–37, 38, 40, 43
control of education, 71–72
Cooke, Alistair, 88
Coons, John, 69
Counts, George S., 6, 89–90

Dave, R. H., 53n
day-care center (as educator), 22, 58, 68
democracy, viii, 72–75, 89–90, 94
Dennison, George, 10, 15
Dewey, Evelyn, 8
Dewey, John, vii–viii, xi, 3–8, 13–15, 16–17, 19–24, 33, 42n, 45n, 48–49, 51, 72–74, 76–77, 92–93, 96
didactic literature, 34
Douglass, Frederick, 40
Dworkin, Martin S., 51

ecology of education, 25–53
education: and bureaucracy, 46–47; and development, 41–42, 43; and learning, 41–42, 43–44; and maturation, 41–42; and society, 6–8, 21–24; as transaction, 43–50; configurations of, 30–37; definition of, 4, 12, 13, 41–42, 53n, 59, 83, 93; disenchantment with, 95–96; ecology of, 25–53; incidental and deliberate, 4–5, 29; politics of, 3, 6–8, 57–59, 60–62, 66n, 69–77, 90–91; popularization of, 85–87; public, 57–77; science of, 47–50, 85–89; theory of, 5, 23–24, 27–30, 44–50
Education Development Center, 62
éducation permanente, 52–53

98

Index

educational biography, 42–43
educational life history, 37–43
educationally significant others, 41
educative style, 39–41
educator as prophet, 76–77, 81, 96
Elkins, Stanley, 45–46
enculturation, 27, 87
equality, 47, 68, 90

factory (as educator), 22–23, 29, 50, 58, 65
family (as educator), viii, ix–x, 21–22, 28, 29, 30, 32–35, 36, 50, 65, 67, 68, 87
farm (as educator), 59, 65
Faure, Edgar, 53n
Featherstone, Joseph, 10
Federal Communications Commission, 71
Ferm, Alexis C., 20n
Ferm, Elizabeth Byrne, 20n
Ferrer, Francisco, 20n
finance of education, 60, 61, 71
Flexner, Abraham, 94
Franklin, Benjamin, 40, 42
freedom, 10, 15–19, 44
Fuller, Buckminster, 90

Gans, Herbert J., 23
Garfinkel, Harold, 45n
Gibson, William, 32
Gintis, Herbert, 19n
Goddard, Nora L., 10
Goodman, Paul, 10, 15
Goss v. Lopez, 70–71
Graubard, Allen, 10–11
Green, Thomas F., 73n
Greenbaum, William, 73n

Hargreaves, David H., 11n
Harrison, Charles H., 60
Harvard College, 81
Henry, Jules, 44
Heider, Fritz, 45n
Herndon, James, 10
Holt, John, 10, 15

Hook, Sidney, 19n
Hutchins, Robert M., 53n

Illich, Ivan, 15–19
individuality, vi–viii, 71–75
indoctrination, 6
Inkeles, Alex, 22n

Jaeger, Werner, 39n
Jefferson, Thomas, 85
Jencks, Christopher, 68
John Dewey Society, viii, x

Kallen, Horace, 73–74
Katz, Michael B., 46–47
Keller, Helen, 32
Kerr, Clark, 94–97
Kettering Foundation, 62
Kilpatrick, William H., 7n
Kohlberg, Lawrence, 42n
Kozol, Jonathan, 10

language, 62
Leichter, Hope Jensen, 22n, 23n, 39–41
Lengrand, Paul, 53n
Lesser, Gerald S., 23n
library (as educator), 22, 29, 31, 32–33, 58, 71, 75, 76, 87
Liebert, Robert M., 23n
lifelong education, 52–53
Lippmann, Walter, 51
literature, 62
Lynd, Helen Merrell, 35
Lynd, Robert S., 35

McGuffey readers, 31
Martin, John Henry, 60
mathematics, 62
maturation and education, 41–42
Mayer, Rochelle, 42n
Mead, Margaret, 28n
mediation, 23
Mill, John Stuart, 42
Morison, Samuel Eliot, 81
Modern School, 20n
Morse, Arthur D., 19–20
museum (as educator), 22, 29, 31, 50, 88

99

Index

Neighborhood Youth Corps, 64
Neill, A. S., 9–10
Newman, John Henry, 94
newspaper (as educator), 35

Olney, James, 42–43
Olson, David R., 32n
open schooling, 9–15

paideia, 39, 50, 97
Parkyn, George, 53n
Peace Corps, 64
peer group (as educator), 65
Physical Sciences Study Committee, 20
Piaget, Jean, 42n
pluralism, 74–77
President's Science Advisory Committee, 62, 64, 66
Princeton College, 82
printer (as educator), 36
progressive education, x, 3–24, 51–53
prophesy, 76–77, 81, 96
proprium, 38–39
publisher (as educator), viii, 67, 68

radio (as educator), 29, 51, 58
Raup, Robert Bruce, 6–7
recurrent education, 52–53
religious education, 22, 96–97
reservation, Indian (as educator), 36
Robinson v. Cahill, 70–71
romantic critics, 15

Sanger, Margaret, 40
schooling, viii, 4, 5, 13–19, 22–23, 32–35, 36, 50, 51–52, 58, 67, 68, 71, 75, 76
school of education. See teacher education
School Mathematics Study Group, 20
Schwab, Joseph J., 73n
scientific society (as educator), 31
Sealey, Leonard G. W., 10
self-education, viii, 27, 52
Serrano v. Priest, 70–71

Sesame Street, 29
settlement house (as educator), 29
Sheffield, James R., 53n
Silberman, Charles E., 11–15
Smith, David H., 22n
Smith, T. V., 73–74
socialization, 27, 64–66, 87
social studies, 62
Spaulding, Seth, 53n
summer camp (as educator), 29
Sunday school, 35, 36
synagogue (as educator), 29, 68

teacher education 11, 14, 81–97
Teachers College, Columbia University, 7
television (as educator), viii, ix–x, 22–23, 29, 31, 35, 36, 51, 58, 67, 71, 75, 76, 87–88
Tesconi, Charles A., Jr., 73n
testing. See assessment of education
theory, x, 30
transaction, 43–50

UNESCO, 52
United States Office of Education, 63
university, 91–97
utopia, 7–8, 18, 33

values, 36, 50–53, 62, 89–90, 95–97
Veysey, Laurence, 20n
VISTA, 64
voucher, 18, 64

Ward, Barbara, 90
Weaver, Paul H., 23n
Weber, Lillian, 10
Whitehead, Alfred North, 95, 96–97
William and Mary, College of, 82
work (as education), 22–23, 29, 50, 58, 59, 64, 65
Wurnam, Richard Saul, 17

Yale College, 82
youth programs, 59, 64, 65

DATE			
NOV 19 '79			
DEC 11 79			